Janel Breitenstein has given e
characteristic candor and wit and her love for God and His Word,
offers hope and encouragement to moms and dads who can easily find themselves growing weary as they raise their children. Her insights are profound and right on point.

Bob Lepine, cohost, *FamilyLife Today*

This much-needed parenting book does not disappoint! Janel's global perspective, practical suggestions, and insightful wisdom will guide your family in necessary conversations to navigate today's culture. I highly recommend this book!

Kristen Welch, bestselling author of
Raising Grateful Kids in an Entitled World

Through honest story-telling that will make you audibly laugh, along with raw vulnerability that doesn't put you under the pile, Janel helps you pursue the most important part of your kids: their hearts. I'm grateful for the ways *Permanent Markers* has helped us refine and reshape the goals we have for our kids, giving us practical tools and guided conversations to meaningfully engage with our kids with deeper intentionality.

David Robbins, President, FamilyLife

Enlightening and enjoyable to read, *Permanent Markers* will equip you as a parent to tattoo messages of truth from God on the heart of your child that they will carry throughout life. With practical activities every parent can do, this book will focus your investment of time in what is eternal and what is best for your child.

Ron Deal, bestselling author of *The Smart Stepfamily* and
Building Love Together in Blended Families (with Gary Chapman)

Permanent Markers is a treasure trove of creative, practical ideas for shepherding children more deeply into the love of God. With passion, candor, and wisdom, Janel Breitenstein offers parents a grace-filled approach to discipleship that lays down the burden of behavior modification and instead embraces the adventure of cultivating a listening ear—not only to our children's hearts, but to God's. This book is a winsome invitation to relinquish control and rehearse our dependence on the God who generously gives us everything we need as we navigate the complexities and joys of parenthood.

Sharon Garlough Brown, author of the
Sensible Shoes series and *Shades of Light*

Janel makes learning God's Word attractive and has created engaging activities that will make these truths something kids can enjoy and remember. The tools found here will help families make inroads into the hearts and minds of their children!

Jason Houser, founder and president, Seeds Family Worship

PERMANENT MARKERS

Janel Breitenstein

foreword by Barbara Rainey

HARVEST HOUSE PUBLISHERS
EUGENE, OREGON

Published in association with the literary agency of The Steve Laube Agency, LLC, 24 W. Camelback Rd. A-635, Phoenix, Arizona 85013.

For bulk, special sales, or ministry purchases, please call 1-800-547-8979.
E-mail: Customerservice@hhpbooks.com

Cover design by Bryce Williamson

Cover photo © Maydaymayday, Suradech14, flyparade / Gettyimages

Interior design by Angie Renich, Wildwood Digital Publishing

Permanent Markers
Copyright © 2021 by Janel Breitenstein
Published by Harvest House Publishers
Eugene, Oregon 97408
www.harvesthousepublishers.com
ISBN 978-0-7369-8480-5 (pbk.)
ISBN 978-0-7369-8481-2 (eBook)

Library of Congress Control Number: 2021935225

Printed in the United States of America

21 22 23 24 25 26 27 28 / VP-AR / 10 9 8 7 6 5 4 3 2 1

To Baden, Will, Corinne, and Jack—rare gifts all.

i carry your heart with me
(i carry it in my heart)
ee cummings

Truly I tell you, if you have faith as small as a mustard seed,
you can say to this mountain, "Move from here to there,"
and it will move. Nothing will be impossible for you.
Matthew 17:20

And for John, who always thought I could.
Mostly when I didn't.

Marrying you is every day like Forrest Gump
investing in "a fruit company."

Husbands, love your wives, just as Christ loved the church
and gave himself up for her to make her holy,
cleansing her by the washing with water through the word,
and to present her to himself as a radiant church.
Ephesians 5:25-27

I found him whom my soul loves.
Song of Solomon 3:4 (ESV)

Contents

Foreword

Growing up is everyone's assignment.

Adulting is the finish line of the eighteenish-year marathon called parenting. Over those years, a metamorphosis happens. Repeated since the first newborn after Eden is a physical, emotional, spiritual, intellectual, and relational transformation. It feels miraculous.

Moms and dads of babies to parents of teens are continually learning about themselves. The "grown-up" people see with new eyes and change as their littles become bigs and then take flight. Yes, kids need parents, but God gives us parents the gift of our kids to help us finish growing up to be like him. Becoming integrated, balanced, and healthy like Jesus is God's goal for all his people—children and parents alike.

There is a seeming paradox in parenting. Our children come to us 100 percent dependent; they would literally die without our devoted attention. But in the end, when they become 100 percent independent, we realize so little was really in our control. Eric Peterson writes, "In ways that continue to astound me, God consistently chooses to accomplish divine purposes through the agency of human imperfection."[1] A perfect summary of parenting.

But there are no perfect parents. Even God, who is the perfect parent, has a house full of flawed, authority-resistant, blame-casting children. Welcome to the ride!

The great news is we are not alone! Everyone faces the same or similar dilemmas. Parents, like starving children, eagerly absorb stories from friends about their own experiences. There is nothing like the comfort of trusted friends. Your small group, book club girlfriends, neighbors, or siblings can be that someone who listens and shares advice from their lessons learned.

But I especially hope Janel can be that friend to you too as you add her wisdom to other sources you collect. Reading her book was for me like sharing a small table in a kitchen or coffee shop and brainstorming ideas like we've done over writing projects in the past. I heard her eager-to-help voice.

Janel is one supercreative woman. She has never been afraid to try new ideas. She's the champion of making lists: ways to keep kids busy, ideas for loving your spouse, or questions to ask your kids. This book is full of multiple-choice options for every season of parenting. It is also full of well-reasoned, God-is-with-us-and-wants-to-help-us verses to guide in every issue you will face with your kids.

While our children are with us, our assignment is to invest fully in their lives, to know them, and to lead them to the care of God himself. Their very lives and eternal future depend on it.

"The years are short," someone said about parenting. And it is true. So I encourage you to ask God to guide you to the wisdom in this book that you need today for your child or children. Allow yourself to be challenged to try new things. Be encouraged that you can make a lasting difference for good in your little ones. And don't give up and quit. I promise it will be worth it in the end. And God says so too: "Let us not grow weary of doing good, for in due season we will reap, if we do not give up" (Galatians 6:9 esv).

Barbara Rainey
Coauthor of
The Art of Parenting

Introduction

The Need to Know

"Dad, where do babies come from?"

"Why doesn't Grandma believe in God?"

"Can men get pregnant? That guy looks pregnant."

"Does everything die? Even you and Dad?"

"Are you a boy or a girl?"

"Is Santa real?"

Parenting is complicated. So I'll do what I can to make it easier.

It was the season we'd been waiting for. We toted stadium chairs and water bottles, smeared on sunscreen, and invited the family. My son Baden, all pale-blond curls and Bambi-size blue eyes, yanked on a shirt three sizes too big and strapped shin guards above preschool cleats. My husband, John, was a killer in soccer; I'm fairly confident we'd purchased a youth soccer ball before the kid could walk.

When the throaty whistle sounded, my son's legs rotated in high gear. We soon saw he seemed to fall down a lot on purpose and enjoyed bodychecking the other four-year-olds. (That was at least one conversation with him on the sidelines.) But the grin, the apple-red cheeks, and the smell of little-boy sweat in his hair? Golden.

The inevitable moment came either in that game or the next—I can't remember. He powered a shot directly into the goal. *Victorious! The crowd goes wild!*

Only of course it didn't, because, hey. Oops. Wrong goal.

That kid's a teenager now, hopefully not smiting too many young women with those eyes. I wish the goals for our kids were still peewee-sized.

As parents, we help our kids aim for certain goals. We make sacrifices in the form of events and practices and particular diets and I'll-have-to-subtract-this-from-your-college-fund uniforms and equipment. Or music or academics or Scouts or pure survival. We cut hot dogs in pieces so they won't choke. We teach them to clean the toilet well instead of disgustingly. We show them how to drive in a downpour and avoid turning underwear a pale pink in the laundry.

We concentrate on the goals that matter in the moment.

But what if in focusing on the immediate and the seemingly urgent, we miss the best?

If we don't play this parenting game strategically, we'll hit *someone's* goals. But they might not be the ones we intended. Worse, we may miss out on winning the game of our kids' lifetime.

How can we make space for what matters eternally? How can we squirrel away life skills in our kids that make them want to connect with God? Could spiritual life skills be as natural to them as brushing their teeth (okay, I'm still reminding my 13-year-old) or putting their clothes in the hamper? (Yikes. Maybe not that one either.)

Enter Real Life: Making Space for the Right Goals

Over sixteen years and two continents, my husband, John, and I have sweated and conditioned ourselves for God's long game—trusting that whatever good work God has begun in our kids, he will bring to a winning finish (Philippians 1:6). Our part has been anything but error-free. Sometimes we fumble and feel far from a win. And our opponents (spiritual, cultural, internal within us, internal within our kids) are real.

Meanwhile, my family is trying to survive as much as yours. There are chores to supervise—and cleaning with kids in the house, as the saying goes, is like brushing one's teeth while eating Oreos. There's schoolwork to monitor and correct. ("No, there is no such thing as a kilomoleter. Or a hoxagon.") There are attitudes and inane squabbles I occasionally wish I could trade in for a pair of power heels. As it is, Lego shrapnel skewers the soles of my feet. And I recently found my teenager's toenail clipping on the table.

But these aren't the issues that concern me most. I can probably get my kids to scrub dishes, do their homework, and maybe even clean up Legos. (If I can't, maybe the military?) Yet, what if I fail to teach them what really matters—like the faith, hope, and love that don't fade (1 Corinthians 13:13)? What if they leave our house of insanity with a prayer lifestyle resembling a stiff visit to an elderly grandparent? What if their sexual values end up more smudgy than my bathroom mirror? What if my kids stink at apologizing, thus trailing broken relationships behind them instead of just random dirty gym socks?

This book came about not because any of us need *more stuff to do* but because our kids need spiritual life skills. We can seize small moments to teach our children these skills, like we would with, well, the toenail clipping. (Sometimes teaching a life skill looks like "Here is what not to do.") We can create space for what matters and work toward the most important goals—the right ones.

But first, let's divvy up what your responsibility is and where that responsibility ends.

What Not to Do (and What You Can't)

At the writing of this book, John and I corral four kids, ages ten to fifteen. In case you're doing the math, no, there are no twins. But a couple of them *felt* like twins. I homeschooled my kids for eight years—five and a half of those years in Uganda, carting them to the refugee center, playing Scripture memory songs in the minivan (#thatmom) as I dodged potholes the size of a small child.

Today, back in the States, John and I try to choose heartfelt conversations with the kids when we'd rather go to bed and let our eyes glaze over on Netflix. And sometimes I hope that all this intentionality is giving my kids a shed of tools to cultivate God in their lives.

But he alone makes any seed sprout.

Author and pastor Dave Harvey writes, "One of the less detected strains of legalism in the church today is the false hope of 'deterministic parenting.' This unspoken but deeply felt dogma assumes the parents' faithfulness determines the spiritual health of their kids...Such legalism smuggles in a confidence that God rewards faithful parents with obedient, converted kids and does so proportionally to what we deserve."[1]

We're not entitled to God waking our kids' hearts. You may read someday that one of my kids is a prodigal. Some of God's children certainly are. My kids make their own choices—one of them may either be president someday or lead all the other felons in prison—and God alone holds sovereign rule over their lives. The spectacular goal of my kids loving God with their lives can't become...my idol. I must love him whether they do or not. Though I possess no power to change my kids' hearts, I long to be faithful—approved and unashamed (2 Timothy 2:15)—with the gift of my kids. His kids.

Catch Paul's words in 1 Corinthians 3:6: "I planted the seed, Apollos watered it, but God has been making it grow." We could say, *My spouse and I planted. All those camp counselors and crazy youth group leaders and grandparents and babysitters watered. But God gave the growth.*

Life Skills Versus the Heart

If God alone gives the growth, our slaving away isn't what matters. We think success must be around here somewhere if our kids would just *behave.* We feel that icy hand of fear whipping us into shape as a parent, lashing our backs, threatening with what could be. In those moments, we are rarely compelled by love; we are prodded and provoked by the concern snapping at our heels, by our performance as parents somehow making us acceptable to God. And our kids feel the difference.

Fear snags my attention to how my kids perform. It focuses my zoom lens on the amount of control I have, causing me to resort to force if required. It swivels my eyes to behavior modification rather than the cultivation of hearts—theirs and mine—that spread and bloom toward God.

When I parent out of fear, I shape a familial atmosphere of fear-birthed "should," of outward-facing laws rather than kindness leading to repentance (Romans 2:4).

My kids' behavior is never enough because my starting premise is one of my own (unattainable) performance rather than the security of God's acceptance of us (see Romans 3:20).

Author and pastor Reb Bradley writes wisely about the priorities, fears, and blind spots that drive our parenting. He asserts, "God doesn't want us to trust in principles, methods, or formulas, no matter how 'biblical' they seem. God wants us to trust in Him!" [2]

But there are more caveats to our earnest discipleship methods, he cautions. As Paul reminds, "I find this law at work: Although I want to do good, evil is right there with me" (Romans 7:21). So consider this my massive red flag waving, my untoned triceps flapping, before you start a single one of the ideas in the following chapters. Our desires to raise godly kids can develop the insidious underbelly of feeding our own street cred. Bradley observes, "When we elevate the image of the family, *we effectively trade our children's hearts for our reputation.*" [3]

In teaching these spiritual life skills to my kids, I try to be supersensitive to how they're responding, so I—and eventually God—can have their hearts: "My son, give me your heart and let your eyes delight in my ways" (Proverbs 23:26). Pushing a discipline, if it's not the right time or the right kid, doesn't love my kids well. It loves them blindly.

Loving the Sweat: How Much Do I Ask of My Kids?

Imagine yourself as a personal trainer. If someone was "sort of" interested in losing weight, you wouldn't push too hard. They may not come back to the gym. Instead of barking at them, you'd try everything from Zumba to speed walking to find a workout they loved. You'd celebrate every victory, and sometimes, in faith, leave a challenging skill for a better time. But those athletes used to running marathons? They'll breeze through that training and raise you 20 push-ups. They'll eat up your Peloton pace.

So we adapt spiritual training in a similar way. Remember that little warning before a video workout? It's something like "Check with your doctor and don't do any of these things that would cause you to sue us." Here's mine: Before training your kids in these life skills, examine their personalities and current level of response to God, their God-given inclinations and curiosities, their motivations and resistance—so "get those knees up!" isn't the only exercise in your repertoire.

And as our kids age, our training methods should change. We move to more of a coaching role on the sidelines, allowing them to play more of the game.

Baden, my oldest, is more autonomous than I ever was (except maybe that time I deliberately peed in the corner to make my mom mad). He's also more independent than my younger three, who ask me to pray with them or read them a verse before they leave for school and will memorize Scripture for rewards. To encourage Baden with the same methods would shove him away from me...and God.

I grimace to think of my kids associating the spiritual with exasperation, lifeless boredom, straitlaced have tos, tucked-in appearances (like Spanx beneath workout clothes), and an overexuberant mother.

The ideas in this book are simply ways to work out Deuteronomy 6 in our homes. They're ways for the Word to be on our hearts—maybe more constantly in mind than the chirp of text alerts or the endless question of what's for dinner—and taught diligently to our kids:

> Hear, O Israel: The LORD our God, the LORD is one. Love the LORD your God with all your heart and with all your soul and with all your strength. These commandments that I give you today are to be on your hearts. Impress them on your children. Talk about them when you sit at home and when you walk along the road, when you lie down and when you get up. Tie them as symbols on your hands and bind them on your foreheads. Write them on the doorframes of your houses and on your gates (Deuteronomy 6:4-9).

These life skills are taught by talking about God's words when we sit, walk, drive, lie down, rise—and posting them around our homes. Consider the Word as a tea bag in the water of your environment, soaking further and further into the marrow of your kids.

In our daily spiritual activities, we train our kids to see God as the engaging, desirable person he is, to see past the metaphorical potato chips around them to the pricey, daily, organic, five-course meal that satisfies for a lifetime. These life skills reveal God not as some distant cloud-sitter but as the God who lives among us, who "moved into the neighborhood" (John 1:14 MSG).

Kids are likely to see spiritual life skills as a way of life if they're just always there, modeled by your authentic, daily all-in-ness with your own faith. James K.A. Smith summarizes two psychologists' work on *automaticities*—unconscious habits:

> We can acquire automaticities unintentionally; that is, dispositions and habits can be inscribed in our unconscious if we regularly repeat routines and rituals that we fail to recognize as formative "practices." So there can be all sorts of automating going on that we do not choose and of which we are not aware but that nevertheless happen because we are regularly immersed in environments loaded with such formative rituals.[4]

And those "automaticities" don't just stop with our kids. As an ancient Jewish quote reads, "When you teach your son, you teach your son's son."

"Catching the Bug": What We Learn with Pleasure, We Never Forget

I loved my freshman year of Spanish. The teacher was personable and clearly enjoyed her job. Sophomore year, I wasn't so lucky. It is entirely possible that the teacher loathed me and my classmates. All of us probably would have rather had a mole removed than attend that class.

But because I'd "caught the bug," my love for Spanish propelled me past La Clase de Drudgery to continue in my own studies, eventually find a tutor, and make a mission trip to Venezuela.

Remember "positive association" from Intro to Psych? It's when we think something is good (or with "negative association," bad) because we experienced happy things when we encountered it. Morgan Spurlock's documentary *Super Size Me* showed that kids who'd created great memories in a McDonald's PlayPlace kept coming back for the food as adults; they associated all those fries and McNuggets with *childhood pleasure* and *being loved*. What we learn and enjoy, we remember.

What do our kids associate with God? His Word? Church? Will our kids associate spiritual life skills with tasting and seeing that the Lord is good (Psalm 34:8)? If I can be the loving teacher who helps them "catch the bug" of a certain life skill, they'll be self-driven to learn and experience it the rest of their lives.

Each one of my kids has taken a permanent marker to the walls, banister, or dining room table. Teaching them spiritual life skills is my way of scrawling on the walls of their brains in my own version of permanent marker. I'm illustrating, even to their subconscious, the delight that is God. If you think this sounds like payback for all that scrubbing, please know that I never want this to rub off.

Even more, if the central idea you internalize from this book is "Try harder" or even "Try smarter," I will have failed. It is God who begins this mind-blowing work in your family. He will also grow it into unerasable completion.

How to Use This Book

Each chapter in this book focuses on a core principle kids need to learn from us. Pick and choose skills you want to focus on in the order that works for you (but do start with identity, chapter 1). Focus on each skill, and do an activity or two. Then move on. Some of these skills take a lifetime to learn, so feel free to return to them frequently, and maybe try different activities. Each chapter also includes these features:

- **Permanent Truth.** Consider these my bullet points of each life skill.

- **Writing on the Wall: Practical Ideas.** Here you'll find practical ideas to implement each life skill. Pick one idea that would work for your family's subculture, listening to the Holy Spirit. Some of these ideas offer baby steps for various age groups, attention spans, and abilities. Rather than expecting our kids to, say, jump right into a two-day fast, you'd implement "training wheels" of delaying gratification, fasting for one meal, or having a simple meal on a regular basis, like beans and rice. I've tried to envision ways to stair-step into fuller life skills as kids age.

- **Fresh Ink: Resources for Vibrant Faith.** These books, printables, websites, videos, and more hand you creative ways to bring these skills to life in your kids—or just prompt them to dive deeper.

- **True Colors: Discussion Questions for Kids.** These questions are for you as the parent to ask your kids. We're all more likely to take ownership of an idea if we arrive at it ourselves. These discussion questions get kids thinking about the whys and hows of each life skill.

- **Think Ink: Contemplative Questions for Parents.** These questions are for you as a parent (though older kids may appreciate them too). They are designed to help you do the hard work of internalizing these skills rather than building a family of really good spiritual fakers.

- **Prayer of the Dependent Parent.** Reading these ideas for discipling your kids, you might at times feel like you're drinking from a fire hydrant (a metaphor occasionally used to refer to my abundance of ideas). This part of each chapter is to continually remind us that salvation belongs to God alone (Revelation 7:10); he is the resurrection and the life (John 11:25). Even in our best efforts, we're 100 percent dependent on him to create new growth in our kids.

- **Group Discussion Questions.** Though it's countercultural to invite anyone's opinions into our parenting, my half a decade in Africa (for a number of reasons) increased my appreciation for parenting in community—for other voices in my kids' lives and my own, hopefully addressing some of my blind spots. These questions help you process these concepts in community, hopefully raising your kids with others of like mind.

And just like that, you've got this. Onward.

1

Identity

Who Do You Think You Are?

My vibrating phone displayed the number that always caused my stom-
ach to dip: the elementary school. And yes, the familiar voice of the
vice principal informed me my son Jack had followed a couple of other
boys in jumping on the urinals—the goal being, of course, to press the wall-
mounted air freshener. (Sigh.) My son insisted it "just looked fun!" As all
urinals must.

But later that night, my husband, John, wasn't about to hand him a get-
out-of-jail-free card. "I want you to come back to me tomorrow after you've
thought about why that sounded like a great thing to do," he said. John
calmly asked questions. Would Jack have done this if he were alone? Was
this a curiosity about physics or mechanics, or was this more of a game? Was
Jack challenging himself to see how high he could jump?

The conversation was reminiscent of one with my daughter, years before.
She was stinkin' cute, sitting across the table in her pink "I Love to Dance"
tee. Mattress-spring curls poked out from under her faux raccoon hat. Being
cute has never been Corinne's problem. It was what lay behind that smile

21

with those eight-year-old Chiclet-size teeth that lifted my brows. That sweet grin might as well have been plastered on the Hulk. When life, particularly involving her three brothers, didn't suit her, we all knew it. Shoot, the neighbors probably knew it. Her grin would flatten to a hard line; those brown eyes would arrow downward; that size-one foot would stamp. And she'd let her victim have it.

Now, I get that she's a girl with brothers. I get that the people we live with moonlight as chauffeurs to the funny farm. What I didn't get: What brought her to the point that she chucked all self-control? What was it about the way Corinne was wired that resulted in a mini Chernobyl?

Over time, the answers to my questions about both my children would materialize as I understood more about what composes our identity.

Dutch theologian and Harvard professor Henri Nouwen articulated three lies people tend to believe about their identities:

- "I am what I do." (My translation: "I want performance, power, or control.")

- "I am what others say or think about me." ("I want affection and respect.")

- "I am what I have." ("I want protection, security, control, comfort, and survival. I want family, possessions, reputation, safety.")[1]

These lies can also be understood as attempts to fill holes—more accurately, bottomless pits—in our hearts. We're trying to fill those holes with performance, affection, or possessions. But only God's love fills the void. When any of us crave affirmation from others, the true desire beneath that desire is the infinite love of God himself.

I am personally prone to believe the second lie—that my worth lies in what others believe about me. My desire for approval—and control over that approval—almost thrust me toward an eating disorder in college. And still, today, my thirst for love too quickly compromises my authenticity with my friends and husband, occasionally melting me into passivity with my kids.

I suspected that one of the lies Nouwen articulates lay behind our struggles with Jack and Corinne. So I examined what I knew about my children. Corinne grew angry when her world wasn't following suit with her desires and when her brothers slighted or overpowered her. And from the age of four, she often utilized her excellent people skills to manipulate others. As my husband and I continued to talk, themes of control and power rose to the top of Corinne's desires. She believed that first lie: She was what she did. And the third: She was the control or power she maintains in our family.

Jack, on the other hand? My son loves fun because he loves stimulation. He also craves attention; he loves being popular and funny. Like his mom before him, he was falling victim to the second lie.

Author Paul David Tripp writes, "Identity amnesia will always lead to identity replacement."[2] When we forget whose we are, we attempt to replace the Object of our worship. And our children's actions and attitudes will always reflect what— or who—they put first.

The Deeper Why

Our kids need our help—in the form of wise questions—to see the desire beneath their desires, sucking holes in their souls. It's why this chapter stands first: If we, adults and kids, don't have a solid identity in who God says we are because of Jesus, trying to develop spiritual life skills will be only an attempt to sate our own hungers.

So let's ask, *Why does my daughter want to join cheerleading? Why does my son need "those shoes"? Why is my kid breathing into a bag when he doesn't get an A? Why did my girl make fun of the immigrant in her classroom?*

The answers are rarely as black-and-white as we think. Usually we're motivated by a mix of legit desires ("I want to have fun!") and illegitimate ones ("My desire to be popular is stronger than my impulse control, so I jumped on a urinal!"). Careful discernment helps us and our kids separate the pixels of what's black, what's white, what's gray: legitimate desires, illegitimate ways of meeting them, and a good mix of both.

Whether to a seller of purple cloth or a cluster of intellectuals at Mars Hill, Paul both hears the central questions of their hearts *and* affirms them: *Yes, this longing you feel is legitimate.* At Mars Hill, that sounds like, "People of Athens! I see that in every way you are very religious" (Acts 17:22). Paul responds then by exposing the ways God says no to the illegitimate ways a particular audience attempts to meet those needs.

Often we seek to fill our bottomless soul holes with what the Bible would label as *idols.* They wedge themselves between us and God, diverting our worship from him. I think of C.S. Lewis's famous description of our misapplied cravings:

> It would seem that Our Lord finds our desires not too strong, but too weak. We are half-hearted creatures, fooling about with drink and sex and ambition when infinite joy is offered us, like an ignorant child who wants to go on making mud pies in a slum because he cannot imagine what is meant by the offer of a holiday at the sea. We are far too easily pleased.[3]

I want more than mud pies for my kids and myself. My own holes—like my clawing for others' approval, my insatiable appetite to be significant and to achieve—are behind some of the worst decisions I've ever made. They have found me to be both a self-loving coward and a finger-jabbing hypocrite. They're behind the fights I pick with John, the words I hurl at my children, and the disdain I cherish in my heart.

Our soul holes determine a lot of our lives.

As I looked at Corinne, I suspected that under that mass of chocolate-brown curls and Davy Crockett hat, my daughter's mind was wrapped around an eight-year-old's idea of power. Practically, I needed to direct her away from the spiritual equivalent of an M&M's sugar high (*Control your brothers! Dominate the competition! Be the family star!*) and point her toward the Living Water.

Years later, I'm still gently seeking to open those brown eyes to the base needs that nourish her spiritual hunger and thirst, unfolding the difference between the dry wells she keeps hoeing out for herself and the Living Water for every true thirst:

> My people have committed two sins:
> They have forsaken me, the spring of living water,

and have dug their own cisterns,

broken cisterns that cannot hold water (Jeremiah 2:13).

If I can locate and identify the leaking wells my kids dig, it's easier to point out these wells' fissures—the ways they don't hold water. And I can remind her of who God says we are because of Jesus's love-driven death. This death closed the distance sin created between us and God and gave his resounding answer to Nouwen's three core lies of humanity. Listen to how God defines our identity:

Jesus has done enough.

God accepts us because of Jesus.

In Jesus, God gives us everything we need.

The Gospel for Your Child

You can see now why every spiritual life skill rests on this one. Identity is about *kids internalizing the gospel, God's all-the-way love, as their source of worth* rather than in finding their identity in what they have, what they've done, or who people say they are.

Until their self-worth is firmly rooted in Christ, even in prayer or devotions they could be attempting to prove themselves, like the Pharisee in Jesus's parable: "God, I thank you that I am not like other people—robbers, evildoers, adulterers— or even like this tax collector" (Luke 18:11). That man's heart was duplicitous; he was praising God with his lips, but essentially declaring his own worthiness: *God's sure lucky to have me on his team!* Who our kids are in secret before God, when they have internalized their identity in him, is who they are. And nothing more.[4]

Throughout Scripture, Jesus addresses people's soul holes. I see him dialoguing not because he needs answers, but because he longs to relate, to help us feel known, and to help us explore what's in us. He knew Zacchaeus needed to be seen (Luke 19:4-6), that blind Bartimaeus needed to articulate his longing to be healed (Mark 10:46-50), and that the man lowered through the roof by his friends needed his heart healed more than his legs (Luke 5:17-26).

A note on this: Finding worth and identity in God—not in oneself—requires a level of vulnerability and self-understanding that won't come easily to most kids. They're learning to cover shame like most adults already have. Time and a display of our own vulnerability form a "safe place," welcoming our kids out of hiding. Habits of authenticity require pursuing our kids through quality time, intentionality, and persistence.

Shedding shame to embrace personhood in Christ will be the struggle of our kids' lives, like it is with our own. Like me, you probably wish you could teach your kids everything you've learned in your decades, hopefully saving them the grief (and, sheesh, the embarrassment). But let's start with basic truth for them to build on: *This is who God says you are.*

Pride and Insecurity: What We Blow Up

My dad recently went in for knee reconstruction at a local surgical center. After the surgery began, the anesthesiologist realized he couldn't successfully intubate my father and secure his airway. But the surgeon had already flayed open my dad's knee. So, like in an *ER* rerun, someone forced oxygen into his lungs with a bag-valve mask by hand throughout the entire surgery.

My physician brother-in-law later explained that no one wants to deliver too little oxygen when bagging. Inevitably, the temptation is to bag too hard and too fast. And without a tube, the air isn't channeled exclusively into the lungs. That's what happened here—and what resulted in my dad's immense pain when he came to. His chest and abdomen were filled with air—far more painful than his knee.

The Greek word *physioō*, translated in 1 Corinthians 4:6 as "pride" or "puffed up," literally refers to a distended or inflated organ—or a swelled sense of self. It's almost agonizing.[5] I've found this idea helpful as I think about identity with my kids because I see insecurity and pride as closely related sins, like inflation or deflation. Insecurity is when we don't perceive ourselves as being worthy enough, which leads to our seeking that worth through a substitute god, an idol. That idol could be as simple as our own control or perfection (identity through something we *have*). For me as a teen, this looked like replaying every social situation in my

Permanent Truth

Identity is...

- about finding our worth as creatures made and greatly loved by God (Ephesians 2:4), bought by invaluable blood, created in a priceless image.

- about forsaking other false senses of self: what we've done, who people think we are, and what we have.

- foundational. Every other spiritual life skill rests on identity. For example, the Pharisees got a lot of life skills right, but they missed the "why."

- communicated through parental discipline by *exposing guilt* rather than communicating that kids must be *worthy of our acceptance*. Making our acceptance contingent on children's behavior only leads to shame. Like our relationship with God because of Christ, our displays of attachment, affection, and intimacy aren't based on what our kids do, how much they control themselves, or how well they meet our desires.

head to make sure I'd made no missteps, never wearing the color red (too much attention!), and forgoing that solo of the national anthem at the basketball game (because, in the words of *Back to the Future's* George McFly, "I just don't think I can take that kind of rejection").

Pride is insecurity's inflated cousin—a sense of self pumped up by achievements, what others think, or what we have (even if it's as simple as control or a false sense of security). It prevents us from recognizing our brokenness before God, keeping us self-sufficient, reticent to ask forgiveness, demanding, accusatory, and defensive. In my childhood, for example, I imagined my grades or behavior or awards or ability to please adults as increasing my worth. I was slow to repent because being wrong meant I was less than.

Pride and insecurity both stem from *unbelief* about who God says we are. And that unbelief separates us from God. When it comes to our kids' identities, we want them to be nourished with what he has declared true about them so they live from that place of wholeness rather than our clawing soul hunger. The book of Ephesians articulates our need to be "rooted and established in love…and to know this love that surpasses knowledge—that you may be filled to the measure of all the fullness of God" (Ephesians 3:17,19).

Making Your House a Shame-Free Zone

Ever told your daughter she needs to wash her hair tonight and had her go all Chernobyl on you? If we see a child overreact (upon honest assessment) when we discipline, the response could be identity related. Our instruction could be threatening the child's misguided sense of what attaches them to us: *I'm only worthy of affection and closeness because of what I do, how well I please someone, or how much control I have.*

Here, it's worth making a distinction between our children's feelings of guilt and their feelings of shame. Author Heather Davis Nelson explains:

> Guilt's message is, "I did something bad," and needs justification and forgiveness. Shame's message is, "I am bad," and needs an identity shift

and relational connection. Sin leaves both in its wake, and shame is what lingers even after forgiveness has been sought and granted. Shame feels like it's welded onto you, but guilt feels like something outside of you.[6]

Parenting with shame disconnects relationally. It says, *You are unacceptable to me right now.* Parenting for guilt awareness, on the other hand, says, *I accept you. And I care about you enough to come alongside you for change.*

This might mean when you stumble on your child staring at raunchy stuff on the Internet, you set aside your own rage, hurt, terror, and yes, shame, and take time to pray and listen. While enforcing consequences, accountability, and a sense of gravity, you create an environment to promote ongoing healing and restoration together rather than covering up and leveraging kids' dread. Perhaps you use a firm (not disgusted) tone of voice or a gentle, soul-searching gaze rather than a searing one. Maybe you have a conversation on a walk away from siblings, rather than with your child in the hot seat.

One reason this is vital to parenting? From the minute they're born, kids subconsciously internalize an understanding of God based on their interactions with their parents. Like our relationship with God because of Christ, our displays of attachment, affection, and intimacy aren't based on what our kids do, how much they control themselves, or how well they meet our desires. *Yes,* we accept because God accepted us (Romans 15:7). But even our continued acceptance and unconditional care allows our kids to conceive God's own acceptance.

Soul Holes, Present Day

My daughter wasn't sleeping.

It was summer. No grades loomed over her. No schedule forced her to rise at 6:15.

To make a long story short, we discovered that her lack of sleep was linked to perfectionism, performance anxiety, and even the potential rejection of her peers. These worries were literally keeping her up at night. I try to express the gospel—the shame antidote of Jesus's ultimate love via the cross—to my daughter, my little achiever, by stressing soul care. I want her to locate her inner Mary—the one who sits with Jesus and drinks him in (see Luke 10:38-42). Together we scrawled a list of the strategies my daughter could use to improve her sleep, purchased a workbook on teen anxiety, and keep talking about what's planting these seeds of anxiety in her.

In teaching her to care for the body God gave her, I try to communicate that she isn't his slave. She's his daughter.

There's a weird tension as we raise kids who love Jesus. How can we spur them on to love well and pour themselves out without connecting those acts to their sense of value, their ability to be perfect or perfectly pleasing?

We show them by not falling into these traps ourselves. As you identify your own soul holes, ask God, *How might I be passing down these idols to my kids?* I suspect the "sin[s] of the parents" (see Exodus 34:7) are passed down not only through a perfect storm of genetic tendencies but, even more, through our own inclinations.

Recently, my parents courageously talked with John and me (even inviting Baden) about their genogram—a diagram they'd constructed at a marriage retreat, outlining the history of the behavior patterns (like divorce, abuse, or alcoholism) of their family over several generations. My mom mentioned their rationale for disclosing it: "It's hard to turn the tide on the sins of the fathers if you don't know what they are."

So weeks later, to my sleepless daughter, I said what we all need to say to ourselves when we discover a soul hole:

You don't need to be afraid of not being perfect or disappointing people. Jesus loves you. So you can do all this great stuff to be kind and love people. But don't do it so he'll love you. That's backward. You are loved when you perform and when you can't—not because of either of those. God loves you because you are his, and I love you because you are mine.

Writing on the Wall: Practical Ideas

The following ideas are practical ways to teach your kids about their identity. Pick an activity or two to incorporate—remembering you're not what you do, who others think you or your kids are, and so on—and give your kids a shove in the right direction.

Show your kids the star within.

Author Jamie Miller suggests gathering apples of different sizes, shapes (some misshapen, old, bruised), and colors. Show your kids that when you slice them horizontally, all their seeds are arranged as a star.[7] In my language: All people are made in the image of God. He has inlaid his value and craftsmanship in us.

Teach your kids not to be an inflated balloon.

Grab a bicycle pump or balloon. Pump the handle or blow up the balloon, and talk to your kids about how when we don't choose to feel safe in God's love, we inflate or deflate ourselves based on what people think of us, having control, and our performance. But because we're made in God's image and because Jesus died for us, we know we're loved. We don't have to try to pump ourselves up anymore.

Race as a family.

Most kids have probably run in a race—and if you haven't had one recently, race as a family. If your kids are like mine, everything from drinking milk to racing to get shotgun in the car is a competition. So refer to a competition, and remind kids Jesus won the prize we could never win. We don't have to keep running to prove ourselves anymore.

Plant a large stick.

Outside, have a child attempt to plant a large stick into the ground. When it's as firm as they can get it, have them or another family member pull it out. Then have the entire family walk over to a mature tree and try to pull it out. Ask the kids, "Why won't the tree pull out of the ground?" Answer: The tree is rooted, established in the ground. Read Ephesians 3:16-19. God's love, the love we're rooted in, is stronger than any roots on earth! If we're rooted in God, we'll never be pulled out by any other force threatening who we are.

Share this benediction.

Authored by Pastor Bobby Schuller, this benediction is one which some families have framed for the wall: "I'm not what I do. I'm not what I have. I'm not what people say about me. I am the beloved of God. It's who I am. No one can take it from me. I don't have to hurry. I don't have to worry. I can trust my friend Jesus and share his love with the world."[8]

Belay on.

Rock climbers will tell you that where you hitch your rope determines a lot of your safety and survival. They belay their rope to a secure point and use a question and answer to communicate readiness to climb: "Belay?" from the climber is answered by "Belay on" (that is, "Slack is gone—I'm ready") from the person responsible for the climber's safe descent. Hooking to something unstable could mean the difference between life and death. Consider giving kids their own carabiner to attach to a backpack as a reminder to hitch their identity to God alone—or ratchet things up a notch by taking them to a climbing gym for a full-on demonstration.

Quiet down.

Solitude, silence, and stillness profoundly affect our ability to detach ourselves from lies about our identity. When we're quiet, it's easier to discern that still, small voice. When we're alone and not working, it's harder to find our identity in what others think or what we do.

Go for a nature walk.

Get your kids outside! As the psalmist wonders, "When I consider your heavens, the work of your fingers, the moon and the stars, which you have set in place, what is mankind that you are mindful of them, human beings that you care for them?" (Psalm 8:3-4). Parts of nature can act as "road signs," reminding us to thank God or to pray for others. Your kids could pack a camera (maybe disposable ones for each child?), journal, sketchbook, or watercolor supplies. God's universe often leads us to exclaim and catalog and create (see Psalm 19:1-4 and Romans 1:19-20).

Try this "deeply loved child of God" exercise.

With tweens or teens, try this exercise from Mission Training International, a cross-cultural training and debriefing organization.[9] Feel free to do it alongside your kids!

Give each child a piece of paper on which you've drawn a medium-sized square with the child's name in it. Using small sticky notes, ask everyone to write words that communicate how they'd describe themselves. Encourage them to be as honest as they can, even if other people might not like it. Stick these notes around the box with their name in it. (It's okay if your notes extend beyond the paper.) These words might relate to...

Roles. These might be words like *Mom. Sister. Student. Dentist. Driver for activities. Dishwasher. Funny guy. Voice of reason. Rebel.* Include who you are on your best days and your worst days.

Traits. These should be both how others see you (even if they're wrong) and how you see yourself. *Funny. Beautiful. Ugly.* Include things you were told growing up, even if you're not those things anymore. Perhaps include things you think you're not: *Not opinionated. Not funny. Not beautiful. Not skinny.* Feel free to balance these tougher ones with some levity, even if you crumple them up after laughing at them: *Maker of best chili in the world. Always right.*

Issues. A friend of mine placed *Single* on a sticky note—but also expressed, on other notes, the struggles and strengths this represents and how it causes others to view her: *Lonely. Mobile to serve others. Don't fit in. Rejected. More free time. Independent.*

If someone has an issue or trait they know affects them but they don't want to talk about it, that can be represented with a blank sticky note or one with an *X*.

Now write the words *deeply loved child of God* inside the box. Ask your kids about the meaning of each word (let each child answer at least once): *Deeply. Loved. Child. Of God.* Sometimes we might believe God loves us, but not deeply. Or we think God tolerates us! Or perhaps it's hard to imagine ourselves as loved like God's own child. Or we might see ourselves as deeply loved, but not by God.

Place one of your more vulnerable sticky notes—to encourage a sense of vulnerability—over the center message of your box. Show what happens when an identity "sticks" over our main identity as a deeply loved child of God. (Kids should see that our most important identity is covered up.)

Explain how sometimes God takes off a sticky note—an identity that has been important to us. We might not be the best basketball player anymore. We might lose our health or a job or a pet. Or we get married, and it's weird not to be as independent anymore. In these times, those subtracted sticky notes can show who we still are: deeply loved children of God.

Fresh Ink: Resources for Vibrant Faith

- Hone in on some of your own idols (and maybe your kids') with counselor David Powlison's X-Ray Questions. He asks stark questions to pose to yourself or older kids, like *What do you fear? Where do you bank your hopes?* Find these questions at janelbreitenstein.com/permanentmarkers/identity.

- Max Lucado's book *You Are Special* is priceless for communicating identity concepts to kids. (Makes me cry almost every time.) In the story, wooden people in a village award one another gold stars or gray dots to indicate their "specialness." But one outcast watches his first gray dot fall off after he begins to meet with Eli, the woodcarver.

- Listen to Lauren Daigle's "You Say" together as a reminder of who God says we are, in spite of fear, regret, and misleading emotion.

- I boil down "shame parenting" versus parenting for guilt exposure in a table and accompanying infographic available at janelbreitenstein .com/permanentmarkers/identity.

True Colors: Discussion Questions for Kids

- Talk about Nouwen's three lies with your kids. Which do they think they're most likely to be drawn in by? How have they seen that lately?

- Talk about your own "soul holes" and the ways you're tempted to find your worth in them. It's helpful for kids to see we're conscious of our own sin patterns. (Bonus: It provides accountability too.) You might then suggest gently, "Sometimes I see that you might (carefully pro-pose one of your child's pet lies). What do you think?"

Think Ink: Contemplative Questions for Parents

What are your kids' soul holes? Here are three tips to help you dig for the desire behind the desires:

- What's the flip side? Sometimes it helps to think of your children's strengths first and then consider the flip side. Could that fastidious daughter have some control issues? Could your overachiever find his worth in achievements (and wonder if anyone could value him apart from them)? Could a child everyone finds so lovable be finding her worth in what others think?

- Look for flare-ups. Flare-ups offer key clues to what motivates and shames our kids.

- What body language—suddenly leaning forward in anger, jabbing fingers, indignant tosses of the arms—gives me clues about what my kids value, legitimately or illegitimately? I might ask a child why tears filled their eyes during a particular statement. What were they thinking about when they said those words, or what felt especially painful?

Prayer of the Dependent Parent

Lord, your image in my kids is breathtaking.

You desire to be Master of our family's hearts, not just a God of good intentions or appearances. If my kids learn every skill in this book without knowing and loving you, it would all be for loss (Philippians 3:7).

Please give me discernment to understand the specific holes in each of my kids—holes so infinite only you can fill them. Help me understand the lies of our Enemy that each of my kids is most tempted to believe. As a family, give us opportunities to speak and believe the truth with which you answer those lies.

Let me seize occasions to mold my kids' identity around Jesus's finished work—not mine and not my kids'. We are so thankful for the freedom you bought for us from what others think, from what we do and have.

But only you can draw our hearts to find satisfaction in you. I ask you to draw myself and each of my kids, at our core, to find every day's rest in you.

2

Prayer

Listening Up

John and I bumped along the iron red of a back road in East Africa, pausing for a herd of longhorn cattle. Our family had been living in Uganda for five and a half years, serving with Engineering Ministries International to help create hospitals, water projects, and schools.

The couple weathering these potholes with us spoke of the path they'd taken to be there, all of us bouncing like popcorn on the road of a developing country. They hadn't grown up in Christian homes, and yet here they were. I wanted to know more. It's a perpetual curiosity of mine as to how God pulls people to him. What was the final circumstance he used to waken them?

The wife recalled a neighboring family. "It was how they prayed," she said. "I'd never heard anyone pray like that before." As if they personally knew God. As if he were there. As if his heart beat among them, vigorous, as closely within reach as she was.

She was in Uganda, decades later, serving God's people because of the way a family prayed.

Permanent Truth

Talking with God should not be a periodic act but a constant conversation that's

- intimate
- natural (not stilted)
- constant
- relational
- vital
- effective

Help your kids see how prayer changes us. It shapes our heart when we're trying to forgive someone. It may lead to ideas of how to serve. As we see our prayers for ourselves and each other kick-start change in our own lives, we can say, "Hey, I love seeing you do that. We've been praying for that!" Praying for each other is one ultimate form of love.

When I consider teaching my family to pray, a quote from Professor Peter Kreeft nudges me: "I strongly suspect that if we saw all the difference even the tiniest of our prayers to God make, and all the people those little prayers were destined to affect, and all the consequences of those effects down through the centuries, we would be so paralyzed with awe at the power of prayer that we would be unable to get up off our knees for the rest of our lives."[1]

Praying Below the Surface

Prayer can be so much more than the equivalent of making sure we dictate the entire grocery list to Siri.

Take my conversations with John. Certainly, there are business matters for us to discuss. But if all our talks concern a discipline issue with one of the kids, or a call from the bank, or a message someone asked me to pass on, I go away feeling like we conducted a business transaction, as if my husband were a great ATM. And he doesn't experience a closeness, the sense of my receiving his thoughts and emotions, or the esteem or nurture that helps him thrive. When we don't speak at the heart level of what's really on our minds, if there's not a flow of relationship, I don't come away connected.

I could communicate the same about prayer to my kids. Yes, they can of course download with God about the practical. But are they relating with him? Chatting about deeper things? Listening to him? Experiencing him in relational interchange?

Prayer should be a continuing dialogue—almost like a conversation you'd have with a family member throughout the day—with an added emphasis on listening and responding. Quaker theologian Thomas Kelly calls it "a gentle receptiveness to divine breathings," "orienting [our] entire being in inward adoration."[2] The Bible speaks of praying continually in at least four places (Romans 12:12; Ephesians 6:18; Colossians 4:2; 1 Thessalonians 5:17).

Teaching our kids about prayer creates an awareness of God's response to their world, *listening to how God might be moving in them to follow him—and then respond to him.*

Leaning into the Awkward

I'm fortunate to have a mom who, at the close of a recent conversation on the phone while I motored up the interstate, said simply, "Well, let me pray for you just a minute." And she did. It wasn't awkward, because this was the culture of my family of origin—and now it's a function of my own nuclear family. Like breath. Like air.

I pray for my kids now and then before they hop on their bikes for school. My kids ask me to pray with them about something they're stressing over. I might draw them into my arms and rest my chin on their heads; prayer can be a point of connection. Just like you might associate cinnamon with warm feelings at a grandparent's at Christmas, our kids can associate prayer with comfort and closeness.

More than any tool, the easiest way to incorporate prayer as a life skill is to make talking with God an ongoing conversation in your own home—a constant activity, involving him as you would anyone else in your home. Read: *Just do it.* Sure, it may be awkward at first. So was kissing your spouse, until you got the hang of it.

Writing on the Wall: Practical Ideas

Considering you're probably already doing a few of the following items, choose one or two more. The goal is knowing God, not forcing something like a mandatory date night ("Guess I'm supposed to kiss you now—let's get this over with"). It's important to communicate that God doesn't accept us because of how or when or for how long we pray. Through prayer, we get to enjoy God.

Try these easy-peasy breath prayers.

You can pray these in a single breath, repeating them if you'd like as you breathe in and out.

Lord, have mercy (Luke 18:13).

Here I am. Send me! (Isaiah 6:8).

Please give me generous wisdom, Lord (James 1:5-6).

I can't. You can.

Speak, Lord. Your servant is listening (1 Samuel 3:9).

I cast my cares on you (1 Peter 5:7).

Not my will, but yours, God (Luke 22:42).

Help me be still. You are God! (Psalm 46:10).

Help me know your ways, God. Teach me your paths (Psalm 25:4).

I wait for you, Lord (Psalm 25:21).

My soul finds rest in you alone (Psalm 62:5).

Lord of all, you know—and you are good.

Good Father, watch over the ones I love.

Make a DIY prayer chain calendar.

Create a paper chain or paper booklet with a request or name on each link. Tear a page or a link off each day at a specified time (before bedtime, before afternoon snack, etc.), and pray together. Younger kids may like to draw something on every page instead. (Make sure you write down what that purple and orange crayon creation is.)

Create a prayer collage.

Cut and paste magazine pictures and printed photos together, adding your own drawings or other objects and textures. A piece of cord could remind you to pray for the friend who rock climbs; a section of sheet music for the person who loves to sing; a dog treat for the pet lover. You could arrange them around Bible verses about prayer. Display it where you'll be reminded to pray.

Make your prayers smelly.

Scent is the most powerful sense to invoke memory. As you pray before bed, rub your kids' backs or feet with scented lotion. Bonus: Touch helps kids feel our affection—another positive, relational experience kids will associate with prayer.

Start a prayer journal.

Let kids pick out their own—and yes, I think an Avengers prayer journal totally works. Keep them in a basket or beside the bed, and take a few minutes at dinner or bedtime for kids to write or draw something they love about God. You might glue a list of prayer prompts inside the front cover:

> What name of God are you experiencing right now (Healer, Closest Friend, Rock)?
>
> What or who feels heavy in your heart?
>
> What are you thankful for today?
>
> What do you need to confess to God?

Talk about what happened.

If a kid had a bad day, talk about what happened. If it's age appropriate, hold your child while you're talking (not unlike God does with us!). You could grab them a cup of tea or hot cocoa if they need extra comfort. Help them feel a tangible version of God alongside them. After listening well, pray with them.

Press pause.

John often pauses for several seconds before praying aloud. This communicates a bit about how we should enter prayer: stopping, listening, acknowledging God's presence. It also helps our minds transition to the act of prayer.

Try old-school popcorn prayer.

Allow kids to pray simple, one-sentence prayers when you pray together—maybe before school, bedtime, or a meal. If you haven't established a regular time to pray as a family, this might be an easy way to start.

Pray for a country.

We use the Operation World app to keep track of the countries my kids pick and pray for at night. (Regular maps and pushpins or maps kids could color in would work great too.) Jack has told me that on a couple of nights when we didn't pray together, he prayed for the countries on his own. Loving that.

Praying for unreached people groups—we use the Joshua Project app—is also a great exercise when you have a map on the wall: "They're from Mongolia. Can you find that?"

Sing together.

John sometimes leads us in prayer through the chorus of a worship song or the Doxology. This reinforces that our worship can be a prayer, and that prayer can take on all sorts of forms.

Get them moving.

Pray while you walk, run, or bike. If quiet time is a regular part of your kids' routine, do they know they can walk while they do it? I also favor kids walking and praying if they're steamed after a conflict.

Fill their hands.

Encourage easily distracted kids to fill their hands, doing something quiet and mindless as they pray: creating with Play-Doh or pipe cleaners, coloring, watercoloring, crocheting, opening pistachios, brushing the dog. If they have trouble keeping their minds on track, you might encourage them to play worship music or to pray out loud.

Like me, you might wonder how much praying is being accomplished. But let's remind ourselves that prayer isn't something to *accomplish* but a chance to be with Someone we love. I take solace in the fact that kids can associate prayer with resting in God's presence and prayerfully thinking about whatever comes to mind. I also know sometimes my kids surprise me with how much they do listen when being wiggle-free is not a requirement.

Write prayer requests.

Let your kids write their own prayer requests, praises, or verses on a mirror or window with erasable markers.

Make music or artwork into an act of prayer.

Encourage kids' natural creativity toward making music or artwork as an act of prayer. They might do any of the following:

- Write a song or poem.
- Play an instrument. I like playing the piano and singing. But listening to music can be a way to pray too. (Tip: Older kids may like composing using a site like Noteflight.com.)
- Paint or dance reflectively, perhaps to Christian music.
- Color a printable coloring page of Scripture (fun for kids to pick out on Pinterest).
- Make a poster of a verse they like (maybe for the door of their room?) or a "poster of praise" that represents something God means to them.
- Enjoy a creative journaling Bible (made with margins for creating Scripture art, journaling, and note-taking) if they're chronically creative.

Get spontaneous.

In the car this summer, my kids and I watched smoke billow from another state's wildfires, obscuring the horizon. I asked if someone would mind praying for those affected. My teen volunteered. We sometimes do the same when we hear a scary headline. Here are some other opportunities:

- After a nightmare or dream about someone
- After an intimate conversation—say, about something going on at school (don't forget to pray for the people who cause anger or hurt)
- When you hear sirens or see emergency vehicles
- After a disciplinary moment, along with a lot of cuddling (*ahem*—no preaching in the prayer!)
- When someone is afraid or worried
- Praise God when your kids have shown character

- In the car, for safety and the occasion you're traveling to
- Thank God on the way home from getting groceries
- On the way to or from the doctor or pharmacy or dentist—for health and for your health care professionals
- When someone is struggling (anger, lack of self-control, irritability)
- On the way to school or work—pray for those you'll interact with (teachers too!), for chances to share Christ, etc.
- When facing a decision
- On the way to church
- When your child has been honored in school, church, or sports

Help your kids pray Scripture.

Purchase the ebook of *Common Prayer: A Liturgy for Ordinary Radicals,* and send it to your kids' reading devices. It includes responsive prayers, carrying a social justice bent, and kids can take turns being the "worship leader."

Pray Bible verses, possibly one they're memorizing. Maybe print out free coloring pages with Scripture verses your kids can pray. Praying verses is a great way to wind kids down before sleep. Below are verses to memorize or explore together.

- "Give ear, our God, and hear; open your eyes and see the desolation of the city that bears your Name. We do not make requests of you because we are righteous, but because of your great mercy" (Daniel 9:18).
- "He went away a second time and prayed, 'My Father, if it is not possible for this cup to be taken away unless I drink it, may your will be done'" (Matthew 26:42).
- "Immediately the boy's father exclaimed, 'I do believe; help me overcome my unbelief!'" (Mark 9:24).
- "When you ask, you do not receive, because you ask with wrong motives, that you may spend what you get on your pleasures" (James 4:3).

- "This is the confidence we have in approaching God: that if we ask anything according to his will, he hears us" (1 John 5:14).

Fresh Ink: Resources for Vibrant Faith

- Prayer walk. Walk around your neighborhood praying out loud for things that come to mind. You can use *Pray A to Z: A Practical Guide to Pray for Your Community* or printable cards from Amelia Rhodes (www.ameliarhodes.com/pray-a-to-z/).

- My favorite prayer app: Echo. Echo is free—they call it a "prayer manager"—for iPhone and Android devices. It's like an electronic prayer deck you stock yourself. Organize and keep track of your prayers and be reminded to pray them. Consider it your own war room...on your smartphone. This helps me to be faithful to love through prayer my friends, family, missionaries, and all the other things I want to lift to God. But heads up: Don't let this slide you into grocery-list-style prayer. This is still a chance to be with God, holding friends and things you care about in his presence.

- A printable feelings wheel. As we come to God, sometimes a tool like this is helpful to narrow down how we're coming to God from our day. It helps us to bring our day to God rather than pray around the elephant in the room (whether its head is bowed or not).

- For a printable "prayer deck" (where kids choose from an assortment of prayer prompts), "Prayer of Examen," Five-Finger Prayer Method, Breath Prayers poster, and 31 Scriptures to Pray for Your Kids, visit janelbreitenstein.com/permanentmarkers/prayer.

True Colors: Discussion Questions for Kids

- Why is it important to pray if God already knows what we're going to say?

- When do you most like to talk with God?

- When do you feel close to God? When do you feel far away from him?

- Who should we pray for today?

- When I'm praying for you, what can I pray for?

- What are you thankful for today? What was your "high"?

- Is there a verse you've been thinking about lately? (Later, you can use the verse as prayer.)

Think Ink: Contemplative Questions for Parents

- What adjectives would you use to describe your prayer life? What do you like about it? What's intimidating, awkward, distant, etc. about it?

- What difficulties in your own prayer life make it hard to pass praying on to your kids?

- What people or experiences or verses have taught you about prayer?

- What are some of God's most profound answers to prayer in your own life? Consider sharing some of these—or simply some current prayers and their answers—with your kids.

- What are some unanswered prayers in your own life that confuse you? How can you talk about prayer with your kids in honest yet truthful ways, despite your own spiritual bewilderment?

- What techniques help you "pray continually" (if you feel like you do)?

- What promises or thoughts about prayer from the Bible are most meaningful to you right now?

Prayer of the Dependent Parent

Lord, I want so much for my kids to continually be in conversation with you, to know you better than they know anyone. I long for them to be active listeners, to bring every emotion, action, thought, and conversation into your presence.

But that's something I can't create or control.

I know you know how to get their attention. You alone create the kind of soil that receives you and your Word with open arms. I ask that their hearts would know you and long for you: "My soul thirsts for God, for the living God. When can I go and meet with God?" (Psalm 42:2).

Help me actively nurture and model that relationship—and trust you even as I wait indefinitely for it to materialize.

3

Self-Control

The Power of What We Don't Do

During the 2016 US election, my children arrived in the US for our home assignment. They watched the silently scrolling news headlines, and the kids' questions scrolled just as rapidly. America had begun choosing sides as if the entire country were getting a divorce (snatching what was theirs, shouting at each other in ALL CAPS with a lot of colorful @#$% thrown in). My kids' tension was palpable.

Outrage culture was gunning its engine, becoming just that: culture. It's a way of responding to one another that cultivates pride in offense (#notsorry), virtue in untethered fury and unmitigated consequence. It's not just anger. It's "be yourself"—the idea that our unfiltered selves are the true and best versions. Or that some thoughts shouldn't be kept private.

What if our anger and emotional, just-being-myself overresponses don't catalyze more of what's right but more of what's wrong? One lawyer warns, "Productive discourse is dying, trampled over by closed minds who value comfortable opinion-holding over uncomfortable soul-searching."[1]

Consider German propaganda leading up to World War II. It offered a single commentary or perspective on news. Then it exaggerated a particular op-ed angle until it wasn't truly news. A bigger nose here, a sweeping statement here. An "enemy" people group extinguished there.

Why Outrage Is the New Black

To its credit, outrage culture—and a general lack of impulse control—gives voice to anyone. You could be a 23-year-old snuggled up to an Xbox in your parents' basement. You could be wearing an orange jumpsuit. You could be an evangelical Christian mom in yoga pants. And you could be a megaphone-brandishing agent of change.

It's why our kids could be sucked into loss of control. Outrage, in particular, grants an illusory feeling of strength and influence—especially in the midst of fear. And Americans are afraid.

As a mom slowly introducing three teenagers to the hurricane of social media, I understand the pull of outrage culture. My kids feel debilitated and concerned amid light-speed cultural changes. Celebs and role models are fearful and furious, blurting whatever comes to mind, even when they're *not* angry. Why not my kids?

God did create anger as a jetpack for change. Anger activates, propelling us to do something. Picture Jesus's anger in the temple or toward the Pharisees, bullies of God's people. But God also gave fair warnings. Psalm 37:8 (ESV) cautions, "Refrain from anger, and forsake wrath! Fret not yourself; it tends only to evil." And James reminds us that "the anger of man does not produce the righteousness of God" (James 1:20 ESV).

Take it from someone living in Colorado's snow-frosted mountains: Anger is like fire. Without it, humans die. Without fire, food stays raw, winter homes freeze, historical humanity wanders in darkness among the world's dangers.

But when out of control, fire incinerates entire homes, national forests and ecosystems, and cities—waging death.

Permanent Truth

Self-control is about...

- treating our emotions with value, watching our "dashboard lights" so we can respond to them (see Proverbs 4:23 and 1 Peter 5:8).

- helping kids, who aren't born with self-discipline, to understand what limits look like and to build their self-control "muscle," managing emotion rather than letting it drive your parenting.[2]

- deescalating before taking action, during the action itself, and within its consequences.

S'more Marshmallows, Please (Now)

Self-control is about more than anger, though I cherry-picked anger because it's everywhere—and kids have a strong justice bent.

Maybe you've heard of the 1972 Stanford marshmallow experiment. An experimenter left each child alone in a room with a marshmallow. If the kid could wait 15 minutes before eating the marshmallow, another marshmallow was plopped into their hands. The researchers studied delayed gratification.[3] (You can totally try this experiment with your kids.)

As scientists followed the kids through their lives, they found that the kids who could handle delayed gratification—the marshmallow-waiters—tended toward better SAT scores, higher success in school, and lower body mass index.[4]

Full disclosure: When the experiment was repeated later, the effects seemed less pronounced, and the differentiation in results was suggested to be linked more to economic status than sheer willpower.[5] Impoverished kids, for example, may not know when another meal or reward will come their way, or when their environment will deliver on its promise. In light of this, it's key to create homes that consistently offer positive outcomes for self-control—so kids can count on good consequences for waiting.

Though some kids may have more natural self-control, in every child, it's a muscle that's grown and nurtured. To quote the revered Fred Rogers: "I think of discipline as the continuous everyday process of helping a child learn self-discipline."[6]

Self-control determines our children's success in nearly every wakeful hour of life: taking turns, waiting in line, or deciding not to interrupt or to spout off after criticism. When they're stopped by police. When they're choosing whether to sleep with someone. When something at the 7-Eleven is just the right size to stuff into a jacket pocket. When they're flirting with an addictive substance, wanting to get married, or handed a grade that doesn't feel fair.

Little kids who can't control themselves by self-regulating often make less progress in school.[7] As they grow, the same kids can be more prone to depression, anxiety, and aggression.[8] In the long run, kids lacking self-regulation show inclinations toward criminal behavior, health issues like substance addiction or obesity, and financial struggles[9]—no great surprise, right?

Self-control involves how we control our emotional impulses in general. It's how we behave when someone acts awkwardly or rudely around us—choosing graciousness even in body language or in how we talk about that person when we get home. It's how we respond to things going wrong, or even stuff going right (like my son trumpeting his accomplishments after winning his footrace...sigh).

As a parent, I've too often used the anger equivalent of a grenade when a BB would do. Being slow to anger is part of God's glory (Exodus 34:5-6). And overlooking an offense is a person's glory (Proverbs 19:11). Will our kids see us return a blessing—in the form of gentle words or a cup of tea steaming in their hands—for an insult?

God modeled conflict management for us while we were his enemies. Acknowledging the fullness of our offense, he set aside his wrath to bring us close. And then he patiently awaited change.

Help your kids listen to their hearts. They need to feel that *you'll* listen to them, and then, with the help of the Holy Spirit's voice, they'll preach to themselves.

Writing on the Wall: Practical Ideas

Keep pursuing a relationship with your kids in any of these ideas, providing a bedrock of relational security. They don't need to spew like little volcanoes for the nurture they crave.

Teach your kids what's better than a warrior.

Set up one of my son's favorite games. You'll need plastic army men and some rubber bands. Set up a few army men on either end of a table (the floor works too). Take turns shooting rubber bands to pick off each other's army men. The last one standing is victorious. Talk about what's better than being strong or powerful or strategic: "Better a patient person than a warrior, one with self-control than one who takes a city" (Proverbs 16:32).

Define three areas you can affect.

If you're troubleshooting a self-control issue, I find it helpful to define three areas you can affect. Psychologist Peg Dawson explains what behavior management experts call the ABC model: "A in this model stands for antecedent, B for behavior, and C for consequences. The idea is that there are three opportunities to take measures to elicit or change the behavior as desired: by changing what comes before it (the external factors, or environment), by aiming directly at the behavior itself (through teaching) and by imposing consequences (incentives or penalties)."[10] Because most of this chapter addresses behavior and consequences, here are a few ideas to avoid antecedents and lead our kids not into temptation:

- Set snacks, video games, or toys that sibs fight over in a place where kids won't constantly see them.

- Avoid the toy and snack aisles at the store when kids are hungry or tired.

- Turn off the TV during homework.

- Create temporary space between sibs fighting—like a couple of Rock 'Em Sock 'Ems.

- Set healthier snacks at eye level.

- Talk to kids about age-appropriate temptations you avoid.

Plan for self-control triggers.

The idea is not to avoid building that self-regulation muscle, but to set up our kids for success, creating calm times as the norm rather than the exception.[11] Snow days, for example, seemed to create weirdness in our house. Kids squabbled and pushed screen-time limits. I strained to accomplish work for clients from home and yet manage every flare-up. John and I needed a snow-day huddle.

What are habitual problem areas where the emotional temperature in your house rises? Maybe it's getting out the door in the morning, Sunday morning before church, bedtime, the homework hour, or the dinner hour with toddlers.

Pick one. Isolate the key stressors. Does packing lunches, making breakfast, and helping search for that single lost shoe again create the perfect morning storm?

In response, create strategic organization. Do some research, and take time to pray. This is where Pinterest or Google can step in with help from parents who have somehow managed to slay the insanity. Do you need to plan 15 extra minutes of margin before leaving? Can kids lay out clothes the night before? Do you need a one-dish plan for simpler meals?

To keep young kids occupied while you make dinner, maybe provide some water play in the kitchen sink while you chop veggies. Or allow the kids a half hour of screen time while you prep.

Deescalate.

Imagine your child skins a knee and begins a meltdown. You could say, "I know! It hurts so badly!"—actually escalating the atmosphere and cementing your child's fear. Or you could deescalate. Hold your child calmly and restore stability and peace, whispering softly in his or her ear. Though you may want to and should share your kids' burdens, extra emotion can heighten their emotions. Try to remain calm.

Remind kids what behavior you expect.

Before you enter an environment, remind kids what behavior you expect: "Okay, guys, we're almost to the store. I expect you to…" Studies with three-year-olds show they're more likely to exhibit impulse control if they're reminded of the instructions before the task.[12] If it's a tough environment, you could promise (and follow through on) a small reward.

Control your own emotions.

Kids watch to see how we handle the big feels. How we respond when stressed out. How they're allowed to respond to a sibling tossing out insults like candy at a parade. How they're permitted to speak to us in moments of passion. Talk to your kids about your choice to control your own emotions: "I feel angry with you right now. But I'm going to take a break, and we'll revisit this." And make sure you do circle back rather than avoiding or denying the conflict.

Make sure your kids get exercise.

As one researcher puts it, "Regular physical activity...improves concentration and motivation, *decreases hyperactivity and impulsivity*, and improves memory."[13] As a young mom, when I'd tell my husband the kids had a disobedient, rowdy day, he'd ask if I'd taken them to the playground. Now we have a history of literally making our kids run laps around the outside of the house or even doing push-ups or planks as discipline when they lack self-control.

Help your kids get the sleep they need.

When I haven't gotten enough sleep or feel stressed out, my kids don't get a version of me that expresses Jesus and his kindness. God has tethered our bodies to our minds and hearts. During these periods, my frontal lobe, which regulates my impulse control, maxes out in about 4.3 seconds. And so it goes with kids. If your four-year-old lies down in the middle of the housewares aisle for a three-alarm tantrum (like anyone's kid would do that), discipline is needed. But we discipline differently for childish or vulnerable (including hungry or tired) behavior than for outright rebellion.

Keep a list of actions and consequences.

I once read parenting advice to keep a list of actions and their consequences on the inside of a cupboard door.

What I like: This approach distances us from parenting emotionally and prevents our handing out explosive consequences like grenades—and poorly modeling self-control. It ideally creates unity and consistency between you and your spouse: This is what we do when our child swipes something from a sibling or has a mouth like a sailor.

What I'm wary of: This approach can view kids' actions as static, setting aside the fact that we kept them out shopping too long, or they were harassed by the popular kid at school today, or they slept horribly the night before. Obviously, there can always be some excuse of why a child disobeyed (aside from, you know, their sinful nature). But if we take an entire situation into consideration and choose to tweak the consequence, we aren't excusing actions or failing to discipline, but are parenting with understanding and wisdom of the whole picture—like Jesus refraining from condemning the woman caught in adultery. Keep the posted list of consequences so kids know they're receiving mercy and not just inconsistency.

Control your own anger.

And speaking of actions and consequences, get control over your own anger. I didn't know I had an anger problem until I had kids. Paul David Tripp speaks of how our anger can often be about our kingdom and what we want, rather than God's kingdom.[14] All too often, I've incinerated my kids and their little hearts. (Know that terrible look your kids get in their eyes when your anger possesses you?)

Our anger rarely brings about God's righteousness (James 1:19). So in requiring kids' obedience, we forgo our selfish motivations—our convenience, control, power, or way. Instead, we seek God's honor and commands in our home.[15] Consider questions like these:

- What is the log in my eye (Matthew 7:5)?
- What is precious to me that's being trampled on right now?
- Am I angry for my kingdom or God's?
- Do I need to step away to get control? What could be gained if I take a minute to get out of the reactive, instinctual portion of my brain?
- What emotion is beneath my anger? (Fear? Insecurity?)
- Will my talk be corrupting, or will it build up and give grace at the appropriate time (Ephesians 4:29)?
- Am I internalizing how much I've been forgiven?

When we're secure in who God says we are, we're much less likely to pop off because someone wounds our sense of pride. We establish this sense of identity for our kids long before they're scrolling through Twitter's daily bashings. Remember the words of 1 Peter 3:9 (ESV): "Do not repay evil for evil or reviling for reviling, but on the contrary, bless, for to this you were called, that you may obtain a blessing."

Legitimize your kids' feelings.

Emotions aren't sinful in and of themselves. But we still have to deal with them in healthy ways. Legitimize your kids' feelings, but teach them proper ways to handle them:

- "It's okay to feel angry. But treating me with disrespect is not."

- "I know you feel hurt after what happened at school! But moping around and punishing your family isn't loving to us. How can we turn this around and get control, rather than this controlling you (and all of us)?"

- "I hear that you're ticked. I think I can see why. What about this is most frustrating? How can you deal with that concern and still show love and respect?"

Help your child to take deep breaths, get away to settle that riled part of his brain, get some exercise, listen to music, or implement other personal coping mechanisms to defuse high emotion and deal with the core issue rather than just the inflammation. (To be clear: Denial or glossing over isn't the goal.) Be sure to return to any outstanding issues.

Don't let them win Candy Land.

Allowing your kids to constantly win doesn't build that muscle of self-control. Take care when you find yourself placating ("Here's a balloon! A lollipop!") or avoiding a character-building issue or situation (like losing a board game)—not because there's a better time or place, but because you don't possess the courage to address your child's emotion.

Similarly, you might be tempted to purchase just one thing from the dollar aisle if they behave. Think carefully about rewarding behavior that isn't a particularly weak spot for your child. After all, having self-control is one way you *expect* your child to behave. That said, occasional rewards are still a good thing for that child who steadily shows good behavior.

Set boundaries.

Do not give in to manipulation, angry demands, or whining. Giving in reinforces your kids' bad behavior, like giving a bad dog a bone. Instead, tell kids to ask for what they want and to respect your answer.

These boundaries don't communicate a child isn't worthy of connection unless they have their act together. But they do show that certain behavior creates disconnection between us; whining isn't how we healthily draw responses from people. So you won't reward and further that behavior. (Adoptive parents may need to explore what's healthy for children struggling with attachment.)

Give kids a sample script.

Younger kids need help turning whining into a question, so give them a sample script: "I'm sorry, I will not give you milk if you whine. You could say, 'May I please have milk?'" I also follow a tip I learned from my aunt: I tried not to pick up my children until they quit whining (which is different from crying). Otherwise, I might teach them they can get picked up if they whine. Refusing to give in to whining reinforces self-control and self-soothing. Think of a lion cub: They're much easier to train when they're smaller.

Make them wait.

As kids get older, make them wait, say, two minutes (set a visible timer) before they can come back and ask appropriately. Then, offer kids a "do over." Allow them to respectfully rephrase their request.

Teach your kids to respond with respect.

When asking kids to do something, consider first asking them to respond with, "Yes, Mom" or "Yes, Dad." *Then* they can respectfully present their point of view if they disagree. One of my repeated famous lines: "My name is not *But Mom*."

Try the lemonade experiment.

I'm personally convicted by Amy Carmichael's admonition: "A cup brimful of sweet water cannot spill even one drop of bitter water, however suddenly jolted."[16] Read Matthew 12:34—"The mouth speaks what the heart is full of."

Help your kids see this visually with a cup of lemonade (or whatever sweet drink they like) sitting on a plate—right next to a cup of vinegar on its own plate. Ask them what will happen if you bump each plate. What will come out of the cup? If you bump the lemonade cup, can vinegar come out? Help them understand that when life bumps us around and we're stressed, what comes out of our mouths (point to the mouth of the cup) comes from our hearts—the sweet (or not-so-sweet) place where self-control starts.

Make a yell jar.

John recently told the kids he'd lead our family by placing five dollars in our new "yell jar" if he raised his voice. "But," he stipulated, "you'd better start practicing, because as soon as I'm doing well with it, you guys are next."

Read Ephesians 4:29 together.

This verse commands, "Do not let any unwholesome talk come out of your mouths, but only what is helpful for building others up according to their needs, that it may benefit those who listen." Even when kids are angry, ask if their words are building up and not corrupting or tearing down. Be sure to include what else is holistically going on in the person's life. Perhaps grace needs to be given. For a printable poster of this rule, visit janelbreitenstein.com/permanent markers/selfcontrol.

Shut off the Xbox.

One study shows a correlation in teens between violent video games and a heightened likelihood of cheating and aggression along with a decreased level of self-control.[17] Other studies indicate that over two hours of daily screen time leads to greater depression and aggression in kids—and less of an ability to recognize facial expressions (which could lead to decreased empathy).[18]

Instill consistent consequences for emotional outbursts.

For a while, we had a "three strike" rule: Every overreaction was a strike; every three strikes meant half an hour earlier to bed. They also lost screen time for outbursts. I now have my kids hold a plank position or do ten push-ups. The idea: Create a mental marker for them to identify overreaction, as well as negative consequences. (My family is going to be ripped.)

Give grace.

Extend graciousness in a hard season, like baking a teen's favorite cookies when stuff with her friends feels dismal or simply responding quietly to her emotional eruption. Pray actively for discernment to know when to lighten up—and still not let her walk over the family in her angst.

Fresh Ink: Resources for Vibrant Faith

- Dr. Josh Straub and his wife Christy's book *What Am I Feeling?* helps smaller kids take that first step of identifying emotions so they can begin to manage them. The book comes with a feelings chart for smaller kids.

- Dr. Straub's book for parents, *Safe House: How Emotional Safety Is the Key to Raising Kids Who Live, Love, and Lead Well* empowers you to address kid drama without squashing emotions.

- Consider purchasing a feelings poster or printing out Plutchik's Wheel of Emotion (also mentioned in the prayer chapter, and available free online) for older kids. When kids begin to implode, help them identify, then problem-solve.

- Anger- and anxiety-management workbooks for children, like Andrew Hill and Samantha Snowden's *Anger Management Workbook for Kids: 50 Fun Activities to Help Children Stay Calm and Make Better Choices When They Feel Mad* can provide great questions to talk through anger with kids. I personally like Dr. Lisa Schab's *The Anxiety Workbook for Teens: Activities to Help You Deal with Anxiety and Worry*.

- At https://www.parentingscience.com/teaching-self-control.html, Gwen Dewar, PhD, recommends a number of games and research-proven techniques to help young children develop self-regulation. But as you utilize secular resources, don't forget the Bible's perspectives on anger—that these emotions come from our hearts, which need to be redeemed. Don't get distracted by only creating good coping mechanisms (that is, good behavior) without addressing issues at the heart of rage and fear.

- *The Young Peacemaker* by Corlette Sande has tremendous strategies my family uses daily for conflict management. It has revolutionized our home.

True Colors: Discussion Questions for Kids

- Sometimes we feel things so strongly! But what we feel doesn't always have to be shown on the outside. How do we know what we should show and how much we should show? I know sometimes we feel out of control. For me, it sometimes happens when _____. When does this happen for you? (Tips for guiding kids' answers: First, we figure out what we're feeling. Feelings aren't usually "bad" or "good"; they tell us what's going on in our hearts. So we can feel scared or sad or angry, and those are all okay. Then we have to decide how we will act and communicate what we are feeling in a way that's still loving toward other people.)

- Let's talk together about things we can do when we feel angry or hurt or afraid—when we feel out of control. (Parent tip: My son with ADHD and I compiled these on an index card, which I dolled up with fighter jet graphics, then laminated for him to keep in his pocket. Our strategies included taking deep breaths, finding a place to be alone, asking nicely for what he needs, and finding five things to be thankful for. For preliterate kids, use small drawings to help them remember self-control strategies. Post them inside a cabinet or somewhere else where they can be easily referenced. When your child starts to lose it, ask, "Okay—what can you choose?")

Think Ink: Contemplative Questions for Parents

- Under what circumstances are your kids (and you) most likely to lack self-control?

- How does a lack of self-control typically manifest itself in each of your kids?

- If you're having a hard time not giving in to your kids' wheedling or arguing, consider what this behavior might look like, if unchecked, when they're a teenager—or with a boss or a future spouse.

- How did the family in your home of origin deal with strong emotions? How has this influenced how you deal with feelings?

- What about your coping methods is healthy and "Godward"? What isn't?

- As you consider those situations where self-control is in short supply, what soul hole likely lies beneath that lack of self-control? Could it be fear or anxiety? A desire for approval, power, or security?

- What's one unhealthy emotional response pattern of your own that you can target?

Prayer of the Dependent Parent

Lord, you know well my issues of self-regulation and impulse control—or even what's beneath my areas of hypercontrol. So much in my home and in our culture works against my kids being controlled by your Holy Spirit. It's certainly not my family's natural bent.

Sometimes I want their self-control more to prevent my embarrassment or failure or to preserve my sense of success as a parent. It becomes more about me than you.

Please be the sovereign Savior of my kids. Show me opportunities to build the mastery of their spirits. I know sin crouches at their door and wants to master them instead (Genesis 4:7).

Help me hit that sweet spot with each of my kids' temperaments—of shaping self-discipline without crushing their spirits or causing them to rebel further, of releasing them into responsibility and consequences for their choices, yet not plunging them into situations they can't handle. Free them from the handcuffs of their own immature freedom into the real freedom of obeying you (Romans 6:16).

I need your generous wisdom (James 1:5); I need your control of my spirit. And I need trust as I wait for all these to develop, especially when my kids feel out of control. Thank you for caring for the souls of my family.

4

Meditation

On Keeping Quiet

If you're like me, you might be fascinated by this chapter just because it's hard to think of your kids meditating on anything.

Well, maybe on Minecraft?

Meditation is for quiet families, right? Maybe those who needlepoint together. Not the kind of boys like mine, whom I continually remind to remove all Nerf weapons from the dinner table. Once when Baden returned from a friend's house, I asked him to start on chores. He begged for a few minutes of downtime first: "I've been hanging at their house all day, and they're a nice Christian family!"

My eyebrows sloped up. "Aren't we a nice Christian family?"

"Yeah, but they're a *gentle* nice Christian family. I've been trying to behave all day."

Point received. Rather than a peaceful, spa-like atmosphere, our house is more toward the bring-a-helmet side of things. Even (especially?) a rowdy crew like mine needs to cultivate quiet, to soak in God's Word, letting it diffuse in us like a tea bag.

And that's meditation in a nutshell.

It's making space for God.

It murmurs a quiet, insistent *stop* to many stormy and demanding things that don't matter, so we can say yes to the One who does. It allows our lives to be lived thoughtfully and on purpose, with room to love God. Meditation is making the choice of Mary—to listen at Jesus's feet, which Jesus dubbed more important than *doing* things for him (see Luke 10:38-42).

The Overthrow of Silence

Once upon a time, I was the beneficiary of a jangling visit to Chuck E. Cheese with my kids for another kid's birthday. And by beneficiary, I mean it may have granted me a little PTSD. Or rendered me one step closer to an epileptic seizure. Amid nonstop lights, sounds, colors, sugar, games, and greasy food that could have made anyone pine for a rubber room, I was reminded that our world's view of a kids' paradise is incessant stimulation and activity.

Where kids used to stare out a car window or run around outside, they now stare at devices. White space for our kids' brains—and hearts—is nearly nonexistent. Even as adults, we've got our phones in our hands *in the bathroom*.

So look for spaces to pry open for time to think. Will, my contemplative second-born, likes to pray on his walk to school. Corinne prefers journaling; we've recently begun Jenny Randle's *Courageous Creative* interactive devotional together. By establishing a comfort with downtime or introspective interactions, we turn mindless activities into time to do what Francis Chan calls "prinking": praying and thinking.

One of the most difficult parts of meditation or contemplation is simply transitioning into quiet—into fuller presence with God. Deep-breathing techniques have scientifically been proven to create more sustained attention, improve affect, and decrease stress hormone levels.[1] They're a great on-ramp to solitude or, at a minimum, awareness of God, even when you're not technically alone. Because I'm not naturally supercognizant of my stress until it bites me (and usually everyone else in the vicinity), I use breathing to help me take my focus to a level where I'm conscious of how I'm reacting to the world—and welcoming God back in.

Permanent Truth

Meditation—and its cousin, solitude—is about letting God's Word steep in us so it can speak in its infinite layers and in its limitless application to life, and to our hearts. It is...

- training our ears to listen, our eyes to see deeper

- paying attention; focusing on God's presence

- self-awareness via God-awareness

- "to more deeply gaze on God in his works and words" in the words of Adele Ahlberg Calhoun[2]

- creating "holy space" in our schedules, cultural intake, and the "messy room" of life in order to think, grow comfortable being alone, and get used to contemplating and listening to God's whisper

- leaving behind who other people say we are and all of life's trophies, and finding our true selves at home with God

First, Quiet

Shooing a kid outside or letting him be bored inside may not seem like priming him for a contemplative life. But it may help him to be a little less distracted and add a little more brain real estate for him to think. As he ages, he can press deeper, sit still longer, and understand more fully what the Word looks like in life.

That might stretch more broadly than we'd think. Richard Foster names four kinds of meditation, all of which I can see kids doing:

- Meditation on Scripture. (Are they looking at a verse you wrote on the memo board?)

- Stillness in God's presence. (Can you picture kids lying on their backs in the grass?)

- Meditation on creation. (See them huddling around some cool bug or weird mushroom?)

- Reflection on the events of our times.[3] (Could they be talking with you around the table?)

With the practice of meditation, we essentially establish a cozy comfort level with the kind of life that listens to God, to what's happening within them, and even to others. We want kids to develop introspective, intentional, observant, thoughtful lives.

You Put Your Whole Self In

Lectio divina is a method of meditating on Scripture dating back to the third century. It helps me bring my whole self into my reading of Scripture—to love God with not only all my mind but also all my heart, soul, and strength.

As you can see below, the process involves four basic steps. We *read* through a brief Bible passage slowly, at least twice, recognizing what naturally sticks out to us. We *meditate* on emotions, ideas, images, or words that come to mind and listen for how God might be moving inside us. Then we *pray* responsively about what we've begun to understand based on meditation of Scripture. Finally, we *contemplate*, enjoying and thanking God for how he's revealed himself to us through his Word, and seek to actively live what we've experienced in Scripture.

Although a number of trustworthy evangelicals endorse *lectio divina*, it can, like any tool, be used for harm. It can swing mystical, for one. Some people, blogger Tim Challies reports, have used the practice to "equate your spirit to the Holy Spirit."[4]

My personal caveat would be not to check your hermeneutics (your scripturally sound methods of Bible interpretation) at the door. We can't interpret everything that comes into our minds as "God told me"—a way Christians sometimes apply God's rubber stamp to their own assertions. God is forthright in the Old Testament about false prophets—people who falsely report that God told them something (see Deuteronomy 18:20-22). We also need to help kids discern the difference between listening for what God might be saying—but holding that knowledge in the right place—and mistaking our ideas for God's.

That said, used properly, I've found lectio to plunge deeper my understanding of Scripture and my communion with God as I welcome him to impress upon my heart and even my imagination what may have happened in Bible times, or how a verse could apply to my life or my past. It's also a great opportunity, when used with kids, to plunder the richness of their own imaginations about how a Bible story may have taken place: what it smelled, sounded, or tasted like. (Manna! Fish with Jesus on the beach!) Why people responded the ways they did. The spectrum of what characters may have felt. This amps up Scripture's degree of saturation in our lives—and therefore, its powerful transformation factor. Lectio allows God's story to further speak to our family's story.

Read.

Read the passage at least twice, slowly and carefully. As you do so, listen for the "still, small voice" of the Holy Spirit. Allow the Word to interact with your personal experiences, past and present. Ask yourself, "What is this passage saying? What sticks out to me?"

Meditate.

Meditate on the passage. What emotions, images, ideas, or words come to mind? How do you instinctively react to the reading? Ask yourself, "How could God be speaking to me? What might God want me to do?"

Pray.

Respond to God based on your meditation. Consider journaling or keeping record of your response. You might worship, ask questions, thank God, confess, and ask God for what you need.

Contemplate.

Be quiet. This is time to rest, enjoying God. Listen for God's response, and live transformed in the world from your encounter with God's Word.

Solitude: Being "All There" with God

You've been there: Whirling into a coffee shop or dinner with friends. Or talking on the phone while your kids fight in the other room (#methisweek), and you try to remember whether you've added salt to the recipe you're cooking.

But somehow, the person looking you in the eyes, or on the other end of that phone call, has the ability to just...be there.

Ever conversed with a person who makes you feel heard and received? Who is undistracted and all there? Our ability to be truly present with other people—undistracted, wholly there—begins first in having comfort and affection from God. Take Paul's words in Philippians 2:1-4 (esv): "If there is any encouragement in Christ, any comfort from love, any participation in the Spirit, any affection and sympathy...do nothing from selfish ambition or conceit, but in humility count others more significant than yourselves. Let each of you look not only to his own interests, but also to the interests of others."

You can probably see this in the kid who interrupts at dinner. Because—going back to the identity principles of chapter 1—if I'm listening to someone without being "rooted and established in love" (Ephesians 3:17), my desires for affection,

lectio divina
("DIVINE WORD") FOR BEGINNERS

1

READ "LECTIO"
- READ PASSAGE AT LEAST 2X, SLOWLY & CAREFULLY
- WHAT IS IT SAYING?
- WHAT STICKS OUT TO ME?
- LISTEN FOR THE "STILL SMALL VOICE" OF THE HOLY SPIRIT
- ALLOW IT TO INTERACT WITH YOUR PERSONAL EXPERIENCES, PAST & PRESENT

2

MEDITATE "MEDITATIO"
- WHAT STANDS OUT TO ME?
- WHAT EMOTIONS, IMAGES, IDEAS, OR WORDS CAME TO MIND?
- HOW COULD GOD BE SPEAKING TO ME HERE?
- WHAT MIGHT GOD WANT ME TO DO?
- HOW DO I INSTINCTIVELY REACT TO THIS PASSAGE?

3

PRAY "ORATIO"
- RESPOND TO GOD BASED ON YOUR MEDITATION
- CONSIDER JOURNALING OR KEEPING RECORD OF YOUR RESPONSE
- YOU MIGHT
  - ASK QUESTIONS
  - WORSHIP
  - THANK GOD
  - CONFESS
  - ASK GOD FOR WHAT YOU NEED

4

CONTEMPLATE "CONTEMPLATIO"
- REST, ENJOYING GOD
- BE QUIET
- LISTEN FOR GOD'S RESPONSE
- LIVE TRANSFORMED IN THE WORLD FROM YOUR ENCOUNTER WITH GOD'S WORD

appreciation, esteem, or attention subtract from my focus on the person across from me. Being fully present with God requires us to set aside our self-centeredness and attempts at image management (more consuming than our phones, if you ask me). As we practice being present with God, we learn to focus on and be with someone else. This skill spills over into our relationships with others.

Practicing meditation has meant being curious as to how present I am in my most central, overarching relationship. The psalmist prays, "Give me an undivided heart, that I may fear your name" (Psalm 86:11). I wonder if I was on God's mind when he penned this one because my heart can be going in about 167,859 directions at once: dance practices and Prime shipping and the niggling feeling I get about the latest headlines.

I have divergent, conflicting desires (check out James 1:5-8; 4:1) too. My heart isn't "pure" in the sense of being of one substance, of being undivided. But the pure in heart—in one sense, those whose hearts are "all there" with him—see God (Matthew 5:8).

The noise in my life chokes out God's presence in my life and affects my ability to listen: "The cares of the world and the deceitfulness of riches and the desires for other things enter in and choke the word, and it proves unfruitful" (Mark 4:19 ESV). But spending time alone with God does the opposite. So what could a "listening life" look like in our kids, whom we're just trying to stop from shouting up the stairs, for the love of Mike?

In solitude, we gradually introduce space, quiet, and alone time with God, tuning the knobs of our hearts to God's frequency—the "still, small voice" he's always emitting: not in Elijah's wind, earthquake, or fire...but the whisper.

Writing on the Wall: Practical Ideas

Read one verse at bedtime.

At night before bed, ask if anyone has a verse they've been learning more about in Sunday school or youth group or even on their own. Talk about it together. Just before lights-out, read one verse to think about as they fall asleep. Or emphasize a different word of a verse in their heads and think on each word for a bit—so that each word can be "chewed" on: "*Taste* and see that the LORD is good." "Taste and *see* that the Lord is good" (Psalm 34:8, emphasis added).

Use butcher paper to help kids think more on Scripture.

Butcher paper is a fantastic resource for teaching Scripture. Trace around their bodies, and let them draw on (and label) the armor of God from Ephesians 6. Let them draw the timeline of events in Revelation or sketch the sequence of a Bible story. If family devotions are after dinner, use butcher paper as your place mats during dinner, and allow kids to color what they hear after the dishes have been cleared.

Work on your Scripture memory in the shower.

Slip verses into page protectors, and use water to adhere them to shower walls that don't receive much spray.

Post a verse of the week on the fridge.

We have a cheapo marker board on the fridge. Every week, I write a new verse of the week. (Or if a kid writes it, the better the chance they'll remember it.) Sometimes I pull out my phone and read a verse for the day before my kids march off to school. I keep in mind the current needs of my family when I pick verses. If we're experiencing conflict, they might see James 4:1: "What causes fights and quarrels among you? Don't they come from your desires that battle within you?" or Romans 12:18: "If it is possible, as far as it depends on you, live at peace with everyone."

Think on a Scripture verse silently.

To change up regular family prayer time, read a Scripture verse and think on it silently for 30 seconds—then longer as kids get used to silence. Don't give up if the first time everyone just sits and looks at each other or tries not to snort. Little kids might draw what they think about a Bible verse; older kids can journal on the verse or on what they're learning about God lately. Their picking the journal makes this process infinitely cooler. Encourage your kids to "soak" in the Word, not just chalk up the chapters. Quantity doesn't equal quality.

Find a quiet spot outside and think about God.

Go on a hike or lie spread-eagle on the nearest vacant soccer field. Find a quiet spot outside and lie on your backs, thinking about God or quieting your minds. Set it up by talking to your kids about verses from the Bible like Psalm 19:1: "The heavens declare the glory of God; the skies proclaim the work of his hands." Check out God's engineering skills on the back of a leaf; marvel at his artwork in a cool tree trunk. Bring a kids' bird book if you want (we like National Geographic Kids *Bird Guide of North America*), or a magnifying glass or portable microscope.

Cart back small rocks (you'll be amazed what kids can hold in their pockets...or maybe you won't be?), and see if you can find which kind they are in books like Scholastic's *Rocks, Minerals, and Gems: The Definitive Visual Catalog of the Treasure beneath Your Feet.* If you have a thinker or future scientist on your hands, you might consider *The Tree Book for Kids and Their Grown-Ups* by Gina Ingoglia.

Up the impact by bringing along sketchpads with art media, watercolor boxes and a jar of water, scrap paper and crayons for leaf or bark rubbings (bonus: turn them into relief with a thin wash of watercolor), or prayer journals they've picked out.

Ask the kids what they learn about God's character from something they see. Do they see his orderliness? His planning? His nurture?

If your child won't be too distracted by the technology, take photos and share them later—particularly how your subject reminded you of God.

Discuss how Scripture applies to current happenings.

Talk about how Scripture applies to current headlines, movies, or even situations at school. My mom was particularly fluid at applying Scripture to any situation, not in a Bible-wielded-as-a-medieval-cudgel sort of way, but as a way to work it into everyday life. From her, I learned that the Bible had something to add to or enlighten everything. Jesus did this too, applying the Old Testament wherever he was at.

John—who's particularly adept at this—might ask, "How do you think we could pray for those people who went through that?" or "Did you hear about this today in the news? I was thinking that..." He'll dialogue with our older kids:

"What do you think about how the government is responding to immigration? What Bible verses help us understand either side of the argument?"

Make a prayer labyrinth.

Draw a prayer labyrinth on your driveway with sidewalk chalk. Looking like life-size mazes, but with a clear path in and out (no dead ends), these were originally crafted on the floors of cathedrals to help worshipers slowly walk their way into meditation. Find plenty of sample images and ideas online.

On their slow walk into the center of the labyrinth, help your kids "release," whether that's letting go of fears or confessing sin or giving God what's been on their minds. You might have symbols drawn—or kids might have fun chalking those in—at certain points to have them stop and pray for things like school or family.

The center of the labyrinth is a time to quietly rest and receive from God for as long as they like. They might sit, stand, or lie down. If they need a prompt, ask what God's Word says to them about what's going on in their lives right now.

In the twists and turns on the way out from the center, they're returning to their daily reality, thinking about how what they received from God connects with life.

Try a media fast.

Talk to kids about whether you might fast from all media or noise on a regular night every week (maybe Saturday in preparation for worship on Sunday?) or for a set number of days. Alternatively, replace a weekday chore with a time of solitude.

Use box breathing.

I find helpful the box breathing (or square breathing) technique used by medical personnel, athletes, military[5]—and my ten-year-old. Kids can picture a square: As you travel up the first leg of the square, inhale for four seconds. Across the top of the square, hold that breath four seconds. Proceeding down the side of the square, exhale for four seconds. To "close" the square, breathe normally for four seconds.

Spend time alone.

Solitude (meditation's "cousin") can be a step toward peacemaking. When your elementary-age and older kids have an argument, have them each spend time alone before hashing it out. This decreases the fight-flight-freeze response and allows the logical, compassionate, and generally more repentant frontal cortex to regain control. Have kids come back ready to apologize for the "log in their eye"—their contribution to the conflict (as opposed to stewing on the other person's issue).

If your kids have outgrown naptime, consider replacing it with afternoon downtime. Kids can spend time reading, completing a puzzle, or building with Lincoln Logs. Bonus: The parent gets some downtime too.

For more activity ideas, discussion questions, and other resources for teaching meditation, visit janelbreitenstein.com/permanentmarkers/meditation.

Fresh Ink: Resources for Vibrant Faith

- Invite your adolescents and their friends to engage in a book club with you, perhaps with a book rich in symbolism, like *The Lion, the Witch, and the Wardrobe,* the Lord of the Rings trilogy, *The Tale of Despereaux, The Penderwicks, Pax, The Wednesday Wars, A Wrinkle in Time,* or anything by Gary D. Schmidt.

    For littler people, read picture books together that illuminate spiritual principles, and chat about them, asking questions to help kids apply abstract principles in their more concrete reasoning skills. Authors who offer thoughtful kids' books from which to draw powerful spiritual metaphors:

    - Any of R.C. Sproul, Max Lucado, and William Bennett's children's books

    - *Pete & Pillar; Skid & the Too Tiny Tunnel* by Jeffery Stoddard

    - *The Great Stone Face* (I like Gary D. Schmidt's illustrated retelling of this Nathaniel Hawthorne classic)

    - *What Is Heaven Like?* by Beverly Lewis (fabulous illustrations!)

- *The Selfish Giant* by Oscar Wilde
- *Miss Rumphius* by Barbara Cooney (on vocation, "on earth as it is in heaven")
- *The Story of Ferdinand* by Munro Leaf ("in quietness and trust is your strength")
- *Waiting Is Not Easy* by Mo Willems (on longing for heaven)
- *My Friend Is Sad* by Mo Willems (on grief)
- *The Sneetches* by Dr. Seuss (on peer pressure)
- *Blueberries for Sal* by Robert McCloskey (on knowing the shepherd's voice)
- *We Found a Hat* by Jon Klassen (on temptation)
- *The Rough Patch* by Brian Lies (on grief)
- *The Goblin and the Empty Chair* by Mem Fox (on the power of compassion, and heart mattering more than outward appearance)
- *Charley's First Night* by Amy Hest (on God's tender care)
- *He's Got the Whole World in His Hands* by Kadir Nelson (from the text of the spiritual)

- Purchase blank jigsaw puzzles and have kids create verse memory puzzles for each other and themselves (puzzle competition, anyone?). Or take the simpler route of tasking them with creating one on construction paper, and have kids cut their own puzzle. You can also write verses in horizontal lines, cut the lines apart from each other, and ask kids to arrange the verse in proper order.

- On a school break, a couple of my creatively oriented kids and I picked out one of the ESV's Illuminated Scripture Journals, along with colored, extra-fine-tip pens. Blank pages allow kids to create their own Scripture art alongside passages. There's a journal for each book of the Bible—so my son chose Proverbs, my daughter selected Esther, and I picked Ephesians.

True Colors: Discussion Questions for Kids

- What's one verse your brain or heart has been hanging onto lately?

- Is there anything God has shown you more than once in the last few days?

- How do you get a verse that you've read to be part of your life? Have any tips or examples?

- What's one verse you've applied in a new way lately?

- Why do you think it's so hard to be quiet or be alone?

- Why is it good to take time to be alone with God? (Kids will often respond with things they need to do for God in this time. Continue to steer them to simply be with God, inviting him into their thoughts and feelings and wanderings.)

Think Ink: Contemplative Questions for Parents

- What are the most effective ways to help Scripture saturate you? Do you journal? Talk with a friend? Wrestle with God? If meditation isn't a strength of yours, where does the breakdown usually occur? If it is, how could you help your kids learn to follow a similar process?

- Sometimes being "all there" with God involves "closing the door" to distractions as we go into the closet of our heart (Matthew 6:6), shutting out the noise. At other times, this involves bringing the noise in our heads right to God: giving him our questions, paying attention to why something's consuming us. Which of these do you most need to do today?

- We tend to hide what we're uncomfortable with: anger, fear, sadness, shame. What do you tend to hide from God?

- What activities in your quiet time distract you from knowing God and being with him?

- If you and your spouse take date nights together, why do you think you take time to still go on dates? How is that like being alone with God?

- Jesus accused the Pharisees of being two-faced: They spackled up the outside but remained far from him (Matthew 15:8; 23:27). Sometimes I'm pulling out my Bible and spending time in prayer, but I'm preoccupied by work or by anxiety about one of my kids or a social situation. Rather than drawing those thoughts into my quiet time, I remain double-minded. It sounds laughable, maybe—trying to fake it with God and usually with myself. ("Here I am! Doing my devotions!") What would it look like to be with God with your whole self?

- Consider the "Prayer of Examen" on the next page to help you witness God's presence and see him moving around you.

The Prayer of Examen

1. Enter God's presence. **Quiet your heart. Be with God**, thinking about who he is.

2. Comb through what happened today. Look for places for which you can be **thankful**.

3. Pray, *Holy Spirit, show me **truth** while I pray.*

4. Pray while thinking, *How was **God with me today?***

5. Pray while thinking, *How did I **respond** to God's presence in my day?*

6. Pray about your day, **bringing it all to God**.

Prayer of the Dependent Parent

Lord, you lead my family to green pastures and quiet waters. But I imagine that a lot of times we ignore them for the sake of what's more stimulating to our senses. Our identities. Our passions.

Help us, like Mary, to choose what's better.

It's distinctly countercultural to reject the hustle, the love of looking good, and instead make space for our hearts to hear. But, Lord, my family needs quiet. We need to connect with the peace you've purchased through Jesus.

More than that, we need you. Stop us, that we may be loved, anchored. Slow us down—and not so we can power full steam ahead again. Rather than what our world values, let our family be driven by you.

5

Studying God's Word

Learning to Feed Ourselves

Maybe you think problem numero uno is that it's hard enough to get your kid to study anything. Why would they want to study God's Word? Maybe they'd rather be at the dentist, with Celine Dion on the sound system.

But have you seen kids naturally study whatever they're interested in?

My son Will, for example, decided that he wanted to be a zoologist while he was still mangling his *Z*s. That's why I lugged back from Africa no fewer than three animal encyclopedias for him to pore over as he waited to fall asleep at night and why we both know the name of nearly every bird that perches in our yard.

Any teacher will let you know kids are self-driven to study whatever they have the bug for. Hence all the books with characters fetchingly named (for example, Captain Underpants). In my limited experience, when kids are naturally engaged, it cuts a teacher's work in half. If kids see God's Word as engaging, they'll study that too. They will learn to feed themselves, so to speak. My son Jack decided the stories in Sunday school didn't have enough detail, considering all the times he'd heard them, so he decided to find the stories in the Bible himself.

In hopes that our kids will develop the life skill of study, we train their hearts to engage, to connect their faith with everyone and everything—from the cashier at Subway to the bully at school to their chores. The point of education isn't just so they can pull down six figures or stay out of the poorhouse. We teach our kids to live a lifestyle of study, applying the fullness of God's Word—and the knowledge he's inlaid in the world—to live lives that flourish for his honor and our good.

In Proverbs, the word *wisdom*—translated from the Hebrew *hokhma*—is front and center. Its concept covers technical skill, artistic skill, even martial skill—and more traditional concepts, like prudence. I love the idea that God's wisdom bleeds into our kids' education because this is his world, run by his truth.

God's Word: The Ultimate Swiss Army Knife

When I was a young mom—with preschoolers welded around my calves and the older ones around my thighs—I was embedded in an intensive Bible study of Revelation, then Daniel. At the time, I tended to see things with (exhausted, brow-furrowed) mommy vision: *What if this stuff happens to my kids in their lifetime?*

That's when I heard a radio interview with Voddie Baucham about leading our families in faith. Here's what stuck with me: I may not know what lies in my kids' future. But I do know what the Word says: "*All Scripture is breathed out by God and profitable for teaching, for reproof, for correction, and for training in righteousness, that the man of God may be complete, equipped for every good work*" (2 Timothy 3:16-17 ESV, emphasis added). With Scripture, they're going to.be prepped for anything life throws at 'em.[1]

Think of all we equip our kids with: Bug spray! Sunscreen! Band-Aids! First-aid training! Do you know how to change a tire? You need a new backpack! Have you read Homer in the original language? Did I teach you how to sew a button? Do you know how to apply a tourniquet? We're constantly handing kids tools for any life circumstance. But God's Word is the larger-than-life Swiss Army knife for whatever life throws at them.

Permanent Truth

The life skill of studying the Bible encourages our kids to seek both deep understanding and what God's truths look like in real life. It is about...

- choosing to make God's Word part of who we are
- applying God's truth to the study of every subject (history, science, art, cosmetology, and cooking)
- planting what will reveal itself more fully throughout life
- studying our daily and past experiences to see how God's Word applies there
- more than memory or knowledge

Still, it's not fear that makes me want the Word for my kids more than nearly anything in this world. The Word is where we find life. John and I want them to experience God in his fullness. The Bible is a result of God inviting humanity into relationship.

Great thinkers, wise thinkers, can see beyond black-and-white thinking into a complex reality; they can pull in God's truths from the entirety of the Bible, science, math, or any other subject. As theologians have taught for millennia, all truth is God's truth. That's why according to Deuteronomy 6:4-9, we're talking about God's Word as it applies here. And here. And there. We show that all Scripture is the ultimate Swiss Army knife for life.

Some of you with teenagers may experience, like I have, the punch-to-the-gut questioning of Scripture principles you hold fiercely. Please know that allowing our kids the headspace to question, doubt, and find answers—particularly alongside us or a trusted mentor—could prove far more muscular than clamping down on conversation. Use their questions as sources of dialogue, seeking out answers together (especially if you don't know them). Fully addressed doubts act like well-formed, critical antibodies for the inevitable future affronts to our kids' faith.

What Do My Kids Pick Up About God's Word from Me?

As you immerse kids in God's Word, first start with yourself. When you get heart-level honest, what's your own perception of God's Word? It's a decent place to start: *How do I, in my gut, respond to God's Word?* Do we see God and his Word like a police officer, constantly pulling us over or standing with meaty arms crossed, just waiting for us to blow it? Or do we display anxiety about obeying or knowing the Word ("Gotta check off that box!") rather than genuine delight and rest in the work of Christ? Do we use our knowledge of the Bible as something that makes us the "teacher" to everyone else, like some overgrown hall monitor ensuring that everyone's in line? Do we use it to demonstrate our vast Bible Bee type of knowledge, rather than that knowledge leading to worship, joy, and love?

Let your kids know how God's Word changes you—not as a project ("I shall impart to my offspring what I learned in Bible study!") but as a genuine outpouring of your joy in Jesus. Let them know what you think about a Scripture passage, and open it up for discussion—as opposed to just *telling*. Ask them some of the questions you're asking yourself.

When John and I served in youth ministry, our youth group kids were a bit of a chocolate box—we never knew what we were going to get. We had kids from all three major education categories: public school, private school, homeschool. Anecdotally, we noticed that the factor driving the kids' faith wasn't where parents sent their kids to school. Their parents' relationship with God was an indicator of their child's faith. Parents with a thriving personal walk with God tended to pass this on. More removed parents, for whom God was a wise religious activity, might propagate listless, barely relevant faith.

What Not to Do

Here's what not to do: Never use Scripture as a club. We all know people whose parents have been so insistent on their kids' spirituality that the kids take off, arms pinwheeling, in the opposite direction. There's never a singular cause for rebellion. But force, as opposed to training and discipline, tends to emphasize not that God creates the growth but that we do, if we white-knuckle our level of control.

We all know the problem's not with *wanting* our kids' spiritual vitality too much. The problem is the way we sometimes go about it. Some parents use Scripture as a tool to lash their kids rather than draw them to God and his holiness ("Oh no, sir! We are keeping the Sabbath holy! Get in this car!"). I know I've done it.

A few years back, the four-year-old of a Ugandan friend brought home a note from the teacher, requesting permission to beat (that is, cane) him in front of the classroom for consistently failing to hold his pencil properly. Now, this rightfully seems extreme to twenty-first-century American sensibilities. But I wondered about more than the harshness factor. What would motivate that child to love writing if *that* was what he associated with the subject? Would he be self-driven to improve, to learn more, if he only remembered it lathered in shame?

Scripture does have a place in discipline. But if we wield the Bible like a paddle, we're not helping kids love the Word's correction or God's kindness that leads to repentance. We're helping them hate it.

The question is *how* we use it. Ask yourself, *What tone do I use when I speak God's Word to my kids? What message are they getting about these invaluable words? Do they hear God's judgment—or God's kind wisdom and mercy (which still honestly address sin)?*

You might also consider your kids' attitudes toward their youth or children's program at church and the engagement potential of the teaching there. Entertainment isn't the first priority. But whether your kids have solid friends and an enjoyable, Word-loving, the-Bible-is-intensely-relevant-to-your-life atmosphere may have more of an influence on their quite-human souls than you realize.

In light of that desire to engage rather than coerce, choose only a few of the following ideas. (Relentless activity, even to bring more of God's Word, seems contrary to the idea that Jesus has already purchased our peace, that he is sovereign and we aren't.) Maybe you begin with having dinner together to pry open the space in your schedule and take another step toward rock-solid relational bridges with your kids.

Let go of the frantic fear about your kids knowing, doing, and being enough and acting right. Beckon kids into relationship with you and a love of God's Word rather than using suffocation by fear.

Writing on the Wall: Practical Ideas

Award Scripture "points."

I award points to my testosterone-propelled, never-met-a-competition-we-didn't-like household for bringing a verse into a discussion or answering questions or memorization of Scripture. Of course, I have a history: My parents rewarded my sisters and me for memorizing 1 Corinthians 13 by taking us out to dinner. Competitions and rewards are for the sake of fun and engagement rather than meaning. Balance these with other life skills (such as meditation) to communicate that the Bible isn't just more to do or achieve.

Set age-appropriate goals.

Give kid-selected rewards for Scripture memorization. My kids have earned everything from a night out with Dad to extra screen time to Lego sets to an Iron Man costume. When my kids were younger, I jazzed up DIY Bible memory cards with Star Wars clip art and fonts. But remember: Action does not equal heart change. Ask your kids questions about what they're learning, and help them apply those truths in various situations.

Go on a treasure hunt.

As a family, trade Bible verses or concepts you've written in code, or backward, with a nondominant hand, or with "invisible ink" (milk or lemon juice, where writing appears when the paper is held over a heat source). Elementary-age kids might enjoy plotting out a treasure hunt (complete with a map or clues) to help family members find the "better than gold" (see Psalm 19:10).

Have the kids draw a cartoon about a Bible story.

Draw or print out a comic strip template for kids to use to draw their cartoon. When you read a Bible story, hand out roles (consider using *The Voice* Bible, which contains parts formatted as a script!), asking people to read or act out their appropriate parts. Your goal here is to help your kids get caught up in God's story. Author Jessica Thompson notes, "I know I don't want to read a list [of] rules. But give me an action-packed story about a good King fighting for his people and I'm hooked."[2] My kids internalize what they act out, and it's almost always...memorable. ("No, you can't just wear underwear on the cross." "No, I'm forbidding the use of ketchup for this.")

Write newspaper headlines.

Have your kids write headlines or Tweets (for older kids) about a Bible story or passage.

Have the kids direct a short video or trailer about a Bible story or passage.

Legos, claymation, a movie-trailer app, etc., could provide the medium. The kids might like collaborating on this with other kids—maybe those whose parents are over for dinner or friends from your neighborhood.

Play the telephone game with a Bible verse.

One person whispers a Bible verse in the ear of the person next to them, who whispers the verse to the person next to them, and so on. See how close to the actual verse you can get when the last person says the verse out loud.

Meet with like-minded women and their daughters for girls' nights.

A friend of mine and her daughter decided to meet with other like-minded girls and their moms on a quarterly basis for girls' nights. They'd have pizza, do a special game or project, and spend time bringing the Word to life (one night they compared popular social media memes and explored how they stood up to the truths of the Bible). The girls continued to support each other outside the group. It created a "band of sisters" who would provide positive peer pressure, supporting one another in the race ahead and their growth in God's Word.

Fresh Ink: Resources for Vibrant Faith

- I love thebibleproject.com, which produces masterfully animated videos and posters based on books of the Bible and on biblical themes. The video on Proverbs in their Wisdom series details the concept of *hokhma* in a kid-friendly way.

- *The Gospel of John* is a movie containing the full text of John, and it can be streamed free on YouTube. If you want to jazz it up, have grape juice handy for the scene when Jesus turns the water into wine, fish sticks for feeding the 5,000, and bread for the Last Supper.

- *The Action Bible*. My kids have literally loved the cover off this graphic novel of the Bible—and continue to amaze me with their in-depth knowledge of the stories of God's Word. When the cover falls off, I'm getting another.

- Friend and author Kristen Welch raves about using the supersimple *Discovery Bible Study method* with her kids and even with their dinner guests—where everyone gets a notebook, and everyone responds to the passage. Get them noodling on it, maybe even arguing about Scripture, and get them interested.

- The Big Theology for Little Hearts series offers board books to start talking about Bible ideas with even your toddler or preschooler.

- *What's in the Bible with Buck Denver*—laugh-out-loud (for adults too) and remarkably wise and comprehensive videos—may amaze you with what *you* can learn from these puppets and top-shelf animation, let alone what your kids will sponge up. From Phil Vischer, the mastermind behind VeggieTales, this series spans Genesis to Revelation. My kids loved watching and quoting: "Caffeine! Nature's gas pedal!"

- My kids are loving the temporary tattoos from Dwell Differently (dwelldifferently.com)—where we, yes, have a monthly subscription for the fam. Each swanky design has the first letters of a Scripture verse, so we can memorize together. That's my kind of ink.

- I had a blast in AWANA growing up, with all its cool games, patches, jewels, and trophies. A lot of programs are still going strong. Find an AWANA club at http://awana.org/club-finder.

- Find more resources, like printable sermon notetaking pages for kids ("My Personal Treasure Map for Today's Sermon") at janelbreitenstein .com/permanentmarkers/study.

- Bible.is is a free audiobook app of the Bible; you choose the version. Sometimes I play it when I'm unloading the dishwasher, but maybe your child would want to listen on the way to school or as he's falling asleep.

- Try introducing kids to a basic catechism. (I didn't do this as a kid, but it's a great way to cover basic theology in memorable chunks.) I like *Cornerstones: 200 Questions & Answers to Learn Truth*—maybe have one of your kids read one or two questions at bedtime or dinner. You might even give a small reward for kids who can remember past answers.

- *The Radical Book for Kids: Exploring the Roots and Shoots of Faith,* laid out a little like a kids' magazine or *National Geographic* for kids, is cool enough to have kids look over your shoulder as you read.

- *Exploring the Bible: A Bible Reading Plan for Kids* (Crossway, 2017) provides a cool plan for kids 6 to 12 years old to experience and interact with the Bible in the course of one year.

- Families with active kids may like the ideas (which may include lighting toothpaste on fire) in *The Very Best, Hands-On, Kinda Dangerous Family Devotions: 52 Activities Your Kids Will Never Forget* by Tim Shoemaker.

- At my sister's house one December, I was charmed by the cutie-patootie kids' Advent cards strung across her kitchen window. These cards from Kids Read Truth have questions for each age group and a darling illustration, plus the kids are meditating on the same Scripture passages that mom and dad are (from shereadstruth.com and hereadstruth.com). The site has other resources too, like memory cards and gorgeous, frameable Scripture art.

True Colors: Discussion Questions for Kids

- What's a Bible verse you've been thinking about lately? I've been thinking about...

- Hey, can we cuddle and read a bit tonight?

- What has God been teaching you lately?

- Want to watch these videos together (see Fresh Ink on page 90) or color with me (using Scripture coloring pages)?

Think Ink: Contemplative Questions for Parents

- What have been some of the best tools to help you dig into God's Word?

- John recently challenged me in my own devotional times to make the goal not only to connect with God or his Word but also to *enjoy* him. How would your relationship with God change if that were the goal?

- What's one part of the Bible you wish you knew more about?

- What are some of your own greatest demotivators for getting into the Bible? What's one practical way you could disarm one of them?

- Jesus used his knowledge of God's Word to combat lies Satan spewed out. What are some of the lies to which you feel most vulnerable? What relevant Scripture verses offer clear truths you can use to escape and endure (1 Corinthians 10:13)?

- I like creating positive associations during my devotional time so it feels less like checking a box and a little more like "me" time: I craft a decaf latte; I pull out my pink grapefruit body butter; I sit in the small sunroom off my bedroom, my toes in the sunlight. After I feel connected with God, I occasionally try to "create" with him—filling my journal with ideas for writing. How could you create positive associations for yourself in this intimate time?

John and I moved from our first house when Baden wasn't yet one year old. I recalled the other night that we'd planted a white lilac bush (whose plastic tag informed us it would be massive) on the corner of the property, and a linden by the edge of the road. I wondered what they'd look like now if we drove by because even the forests of Colorado—pillars of an ecosystem—began as seeds.

Maybe that's what I love about this life skill. It's about planting something living and active, something stretching into nurturing trees that outgrow me (Matthew 13:31-32).

Prayer of the Dependent Parent

Lord, I want my kids to taste and see that you're good (Psalm 34:8). But it's a decent challenge to help someone else fall in love with your Word, particularly when I have no power to change what's in them. Remind me that my kids' Bible knowledge is not my merit badge. My kids' or my own spiritual résumé is trash in light of knowing you (Philippians 3:4-9).

Reveal my attitude toward your truth—whether I let it transform me, whether I see it as beautiful, whether I fully believe it to be true.

Show me opportunities to bring Scripture into all the little and big moments with my kids. Create in me a thirst to listen to you through your Word and do what it says (James 1:22). Shape my kids to be fierce, devoted lovers of the Bible who determine all truth through its lens, cherish it, and depend on it for the words of life (John 6:68).

6

Simplicity

When Less Is So Much More

The window of time with Baden at home keeps shrinking despite my longing to prop it open, its gravity threatening to pinch my heart at the end. But adulting's gotta happen. So we asked Baden to draw up a clothing budget for the year, then doled out a corresponding clothing allowance (plus a little extra for whatever he didn't anticipate).

When I later suggested he purchase another pair of shoes, imagine the lift of my eyebrows when he responded, "No, thanks." He shrugged. "Just don't need 'em. Trying to live simply, ya know?"

I'd think Corinne would live differently, but lately even she has been lobbing garbage bags of used clothes that land with a *thwap* by the door. She doesn't like the clutter, the maintenance of keeping sleeves from dangling out of dresser drawers. We set bins in our kids' rooms, asking the kids to pile them with whatever they're not using. Sometimes I'm surprised, or maybe even saddened, at what ends up in them because I thought surely they would have loved that Christmas gift or been more excited about that microscope.

But it's not horrible, I reason with myself, that they understand buyer's remorse, that they understand the fickle gremlins of human emotion and desire. So I have to talk with my kids about the microscope with its fuzz of dust, the shirt they love-love-loved for about 4.7 weeks. Until they didn't. For Baden, it means he's not shelling out for another Nike hoodie anytime soon, since a wayward welding spark from shop class melted a hole in it, and he's decided he doesn't like the fit anyway. He's living a little wiser, I think, and a little simpler.

In his book *The Treasure Principle*, Randy Alcorn explains, "The more things we own—the greater their total mass—the more they grip us, setting us in orbit around them."[1] We sense this: our hearts and longing tangled up with where our treasure is. Beneath the "treasure" itself, there's greater treasure we want: acceptance, comfort, and self-value. The holes in our hearts are never truly filled by more stuff, more food, more *doing*.

But isn't it ironic we have to fight so hard for a shred of simplicity?

Richard Foster observes,

> To attempt to arrange an outward life-style of simplicity without the inward reality leads to deadly legalism.
>
> Simplicity begins in inward focus and unity…Experiencing the inward reality liberates us outwardly. Speech becomes truthful and honest. The lust for status and position is gone because we no longer need status and position. We cease from showy extravagance not on the grounds of being unable to afford it, but on the grounds of principle. Our goods become available to others. We join the experience that Richard E. Byrd, after months alone in the barren Arctic, recorded in his journal, "I am learning…that a man can live profoundly without masses of things."[2]

Simplicity is a form of fasting, a way of choosing the contentment God offers us (Philippians 4:12-13). It's cutting out the cheese puffs portion (that is, a lot of air garnished with some unnaturally nuclear-orange flavoring) of our belongings, our schedule, our talk, and our preoccupations that connive us into thinking we're nourished, full, and happy.

Permanent Truth

Simplicity and its sibling, fasting, are about finding freedom, joy, an undivided heart, and gut-level satisfaction in lives untethered by excess. We can train our minds and hearts away from our constant appetites and the idea that *more* equals happiness, comfort, and convenience. It is about quieting the "background noise" that prevents us from hearing God. And it's about freeing ourselves from the chokehold of materialism, pleasure-seeking, and anxiety (Luke 8:14).

Fasting is a sweet offering to God of choosing *against* something we really like or crave for a little while so we can be satisfied by him—our true feast—rather than all the pleasures in our lives. Fasting chooses to snip the ties of habits that control us. It learns to appreciate the Giver more than our gifts.

Pastor Johnathon Bowers believes that gluttony, "America's most tolerated sin," is "more about the direction of our loves than it is about the contents of our cupboards."[3] Before living in Uganda, I probably would have told you this didn't apply to me. John and I were often scraping to care for four kids on a single income. But if simplicity is more about our hearts' contentment, perhaps the number of zeros in our income is less important. I knew plenty of people in poverty who, like me, struggled with the same issues of greed and trust in possessions. Small quantities can still snare any of us with selfishness, impatience, a lack of surrender.

American Dream or American Lie?

Living overseas and developing cross-cultural friendships, I discovered our cultures each have their own soul holes, their own lies about where fulfillment can be realized. Each has some version of "If you_____, your life will sing." The amassing of wealth and possessions seems to be as American as apple pie. We live in a state of superabundance, only occasionally peering out on the way 80 percent of the world lives in poverty.

Yes, our wealth propels us toward greater comfort, greater self-actualization, and the ability to change our circumstances. The rest of the world generally finds this enviable, to say the least. But our stuff and schedules and isolating cultural noise can sate us to the point of forgetting that our true hunger lies much deeper. There's only one Bread that satisfies.

Perhaps that's why many celebrities who've reached the pinnacle of the American dream carry terrifyingly high divorce and suicide rates. At the top of this ladder, there's nothing fulfilling. Those the most full of our society's prime fare are still startlingly famished.

But while I like to think I'm clear-eyed about the emptiness of worldly gain, sometimes my view of God's favor—of being "#blessed"—can be very prescriptive. Sometimes it's a thinly veiled version of the American dream.

Let's look at how the Bible describes God's favor. Gabriel, for example, described Mary as "highly favored! The Lord is with you" (Luke 1:28). From the overview of this "highly favored" woman's life, maybe we'd arch our eyebrows.

You, an unwed mother, will live in the shame of your community. You will flee the country to avoid your son's intended infanticide, but your friends won't make it out. Your son will die of the sickest form of capital punishment. But not before you've wondered if he's gone off the deep end. Oh, and you will live in poverty, as will your son. Your cousin's son will also be executed unjustly, and another one of your sons will also be tortured to death.

Mary's blessed life was also pierced.

Yes, God's favor often shows up in the form of a needed vehicle or a lovely home or the shower drain suddenly clearing so you don't have to call the plumber.

Sometimes, it doesn't. Sometimes, as Jesus reminds us in the story of the rich young ruler, our prosperity stands between us and the only thing that matters. It's possible for any one of us to gain the whole world, yet lose our soul (Mark 8:36). This is also shown in verses like "Watch out! Be on your guard against all kinds of greed; life does not consist in an abundance of possessions" (Luke 12:15), or "You cannot serve both God and money" (Matthew 6:24).

Some of the most contented people I've met have been some of the poorest on this planet. I tell you this to illustrate two pearls that Africa has folded into my palms with her own mahogany-colored hands: the gift—the sheer joy—of simplicity, with a side of global and historical perspective.

I will never come close to the ability of so many Africans to survive on so little. My dear friend—following the death of both parents from AIDS and subsequently being thrown out by her stepmom—put her four brothers and sisters through school by working in terrible conditions...and then decided to adopt twins she found on a pile of trash. She could outfast and outlast me in hardship any day of the week. But living with less left my heart leaner and more sinewy. It slowly sliced off the fat I'd brought with me: "Let us throw off everything that hinders and the sin that so easily entangles" (Hebrews 12:1).

My family and I are still working out what this means in America. We decided to purchase a smaller home with less storage so we'd have to purge and streamline our spaces. That means my three boys share a room. Corinne's doubles as a guest room. Sometimes it means less space to host. But overall, we like it.

Simplicity for us can also mean whittling down our meals to one or two courses or consuming less meat—like the rest of the world. It could mean simpler gift-giving and a lot of concerted effort toward gratitude. It sometimes means looking the other way when there's a killer sale on something I don't need. (The community garage sale is my kryptonite.) It means constant purging, seeing if we can do without, fixing rather than buying new, and restricting our budget to buy less than we might afford. Yet, whatever form "less" takes, it's almost always more.

Fasting

One form of less is fasting. It's hard enough for us as adults to get the idea behind fasting, so it may be hard to imagine asking it of our kids. I also sometimes laugh that fasting makes me more sinful: sniping at the kids, my malnourished capacity for obstacles reduced to that of a two-year-old.

But I like how John Piper approaches fasting: It is about demonstrating a hunger for God.[4] It's like saying, *God, I want you this much. I recognize I don't live on food alone.*

God made life's pleasures as good gifts. First Timothy 4:4 tells us, "Everything God created is good, and nothing is to be rejected if it is received with thanksgiving." But God never meant those gifts to satisfy us, to edge out our hunger for him. Fasting helps us step away from temporary satisfactions so we can spend time thinking of him and praying more.

Earlier in this book, I mentioned my kids haven't engaged in all the ideas of this book—and this is an example. With our particular kids and family composition, we've focused more on simplicity than fasting. (For one thing, because blood sugar levels have a direct correlation to my own kids' behavior, this seems to fall into the category of "to obey is better than sacrifice" [1 Samuel 15:22].) So you could say we've stuck to the training wheels of this discipline—all-family media fasts, fasting from phones, eating beans and rice for a night, and intentionally going without items.

I like the disciplines of simplicity and fasting as a family to be driven by my kids' engagement so they have ownership. That way, the hard moments aren't seen as "parents and God versus Me." Explain that fasting and simplicity are about training ourselves to hunger for what really matters—for the greater reward of appetites steered toward what we can't see. God is our true feast. More than about what we're giving up, fasting and simplicity align with other themes in the Bible: We sacrifice now for the joy of what's later. Jesus did this when he went to the cross for the joy set before him (Hebrews 12:2).

What Fasting Isn't

Because lack of food can interfere with school, attention, and behavior, my thought is not to expect kids to fast during school days. Summer, school breaks, and weekends work better. If you're considering inviting your children to fast during school days, it may be best to ease in with fasting from a particular food. Or perhaps you could decide together to fast from the evening meal, then eat a full breakfast before school. Ask your kids when they would like to fast; buy-in and ownership of this are your friends.

Because many people have different notions of fasting, it is important to note what fasting is not.

Fasting is not focused on achievement. It "is a quiet event shared only by two."[5] This is a great time to talk with our kids about self-righteousness and serving God privately. If we quietly think ourselves a better family because we fast, we're actually worshipping ourselves (see Colossians 2:20-23). Though our kids' discipline is something to encourage and praise, ultimately, the goal of fasting isn't their achievement, but enjoyment of and focus on God.

Fasting is not to make God produce something. Pleading with God for something through fasting is biblical (see Esther 4:16; Daniel 9:3-5; 2 Samuel 12:15-17; and Acts 14:23, for starters). Yet this is different from "I fasted, so God should do _____ for me." That's a spiritualized form of entitlement and even dependence on our own acts of righteousness (ironically the opposite of the humility and hands-off-ness we're going for).

Fasting is not an immediate spiritual high. It's more like starting an exercise program, say the authors of *Habits of a Child's Heart.* It takes a while for fasting to feel effective, meaningful.

Meanwhile, in a "fast" for our house, John and I keep filling trash bags with things and lobbing them to the bottom of the stairs. We're withdrawing items from our schedule, like gorillas removing insects from fur. Less hurry. Less fuss. Less glitz. Less fluff.

More life.

Writing on the Wall: Practical Ideas

For kids who have food issues (food hoarding, tendencies toward eating disorders, etc.), consider saving this skill for a different season in life when their spirituality won't be unnecessarily tangled in those complexities.

Let go of any fear-parenting that might drive you to be better, do better, or look better, and pick one or two activities that are right for your family in this season.

Simplify your meals.

Aim for meals with fewer courses, fewer dishes, less time. I come from generations of people who enjoy large, happy meals together, which has shown me the value of the family table and the true fellowship of breaking bread. But for my family, sometimes big meals have been just...more. (The Mennonite cookbook *More-with-Less* reminds me I can make simpler recipes that consume less of the world's resources.) John has asked for fewer hot breakfasts for our kids—and fewer dishes and less chaos and hurry from me in the mornings. I'm trying to strike a balance between creating a sense of home and a prepared place—as a taste of what God does for us; see John 14:2—with actual presence with my kids.

Give up sugar, snacks, or dessert one day a week.

God, instead, is your treat. You might sing songs at the end of dinner. You can then work up to a span of several days or even weeks.

Relentlessly streamline chaos.

Turn off the TV or music in the car, during meals, or while you're milling around the house; plan the TV shows you will watch, and turn off the TV the rest of the time. Get a firm rein on kids' screen time. Plan your grocery list, and "fast" from buying tempting little extras. *(Do we need five kinds of salad dressing?)*

Reduce extracurricular activities.

Maybe this looks like one activity per child or even fewer programmed church activities. Help kids adapt to the pace of a "three mile an hour God"[6] by simplifying your family calendar—especially in prep for Sunday worship, but throughout the week too. Create glorious white space on the calendar, creating time for kids to think or run around outside; to relax together without anything on the calendar; to wedge in time for childhood (and adulthood) joy.

Organize your cupboards and the fridge.

Did you know Americans discard up to 40 percent of their food? Our disorganization led to things like having more than one container open of the same food and buying more when forgetting we'd already purchased something. Getting the kids on board, we set a goal to reduce our grocery budget by ten percent. A compost bucket increases our awareness of wasted food. We're eating on smaller plates too, which means smaller servings. Cleaner cupboards and more essential food make me feel like I can fill my lungs all the way again.

Put off gratification.

Delay your online order or grocery shopping. Live off what you have. Shop from your pantry, creating meals from what you have rather than those that will require buying more ingredients.

Talk with your kids about one thing they could give up for a period of time.

Possibilities could include meat, social media, makeup, TV, buying something for self, complaining. Challenge them one step beyond what's easy for them. The idea is not to offer sacrifices that cost us nothing (2 Samuel 24:24) but to be a cheerful giver who doesn't give out of obligation (2 Corinthians 9:6-7).

Simplify family wardrobes.

Set a large plastic bin in a child's room. Ask them to fill it with as many unneeded toys and clothes as they can. Or have a slim-down-your-room contest between kids. This discipline can be a form of both simplicity and fasting. Here are a few tips:

- Operate by the "one in, one out" principle. If kids acquire new clothing, consider asking them to give an equal amount away.

- Give away what's not an "A." Is it at the top of the class in quality, age-appropriateness, fit (yes, now), versatility, style, color, preference, and maintenance?

- If you haven't worn it in a year, you probably don't need it.

- More than one type of some items—with exceptions like shirts, socks, underwear, and jeans—is probably more than needed.
- Keep donation bags in your closets for constant weeding out.

Help your kids keep their commitments to God.

If your family is fasting from food, encourage them with a note card on the fridge or TV ("So proud of you. Keep it up!") or a text ("Just a reminder that six hours are left in our meat fast. Keep going! Almost there! [insert Bible verse] Proud of you for choosing this for God.").

Consider weaning yourself off caffeine.

Second Peter reminds us that "people are slaves to whatever has mastered them" (2:19)—and you might like life untethered from *Must. Have. Coffee.* (If your doctor approves, green tea or a vitamin B supplement may provide less addictive energy boosts on sleepy days.)

Fresh Ink: Resources for Vibrant Faith

Simplicity is countercultural enough that it may require some adult books to help you alter your own family's subculture.

- *Raising Grateful Kids in an Entitled World: How One Family Learned That Saying No Can Lead to Life's Biggest Yes* is chock-full of ways to alter kids' perspective and get them excited about serving. And if your family wants to fast from comfort and move toward advocating for justice, author Kristen Welch has posted "100+ Ways for Your Family to Make a Difference" on her blog.
- Pastor John Mark Comer's *The Ruthless Elimination of Hurry: How to Stay Emotionally Healthy and Spiritually Alive in the Chaos of the Modern World* offers wise advice on a simpler, slower pace of life for a family, starting with you.
- Consider sponsoring a child as a family—and becoming his or her

pen pal—through Lahash.org or Compassion.com. Compassion also publishes their own kids' magazine.

- The children's book *One Potato, Two Potato* by Cynthia DeFelice teaches valuable contentment.

- Together, watch movies like *Queen of Katwe* or *The Boy Who Harnessed the Wind* to glimpse the lives of characters your kids' age who live in poverty.

- Find 20 ideas to speak the "love language" of gift-giving without doing it more elaborately at janelbreitenstein.com/permanentmarkers /simplicity. I've also posted my closest Ugandan friend Olivia's smash-hit beans and rice recipe for our family.

True Colors: Discussion Questions for Kids

Up the ante by having these conversations after watching kids' videos on Com passion.com, seeing a movie like *Queen of Katwe* or *The Boy Who Harnessed the Wind*, or taking your kids with you to serve in a poorer area of town.

- Sometimes activities or stuff or food gets in the way of our remembering that none of those things satisfy us inside. What's one thing you would be willing to give up for a while, or maybe once a week, to remind you that we don't need those things to be satisfied? (Give your kids a few ideas, and tell them what you personally are giving up.)

- What's something you make a little too important sometimes? (Video games? Movie night? Your phone?) What could it look like to step away from that for a while?

- Have you ever become stronger because of something you've done without?

- Why do you think Jesus fasted for 40 days before he began his ministry? Do you think this made him stronger or weaker for his temptation by Satan?

Think Ink: Contemplative Questions for Parents

- What areas of your family's lives feel harried?

- Do the pace and priorities of your life accurately express your desired values?

- What systems could you put in place to keep your schedule serving you and promoting peace and presence, rather than the opposite?

- How could you fast from your constant "yes" to the opportunities before you? What values do you—yourself and as a family—want to determine your family's schedule, rather than the other way around? What would it look like to create margin, emotional energy, and a culture of rest and essentialism in your home, to "ruthlessly eliminate hurry from your life"?[7]

- What behavior could you fast from? God tells the Israelites,

> Is not this the kind of fasting I have chosen:
> to loose the chains of injustice
>   and untie the cords of the yoke,
> to set the oppressed free
>   and break every yoke?
> Is it not to share your food with the hungry
>   and to provide the poor wanderer with shelter—
> when you see the naked, to clothe them,
>   and not to turn away from your own flesh and blood? (Isaiah 58:6-7).

Prayer of the Dependent Parent

Lord, you've said that where my treasure is, my heart is (Matthew 6:21). What do you want to reveal about where my heart is?

It's hard to discern your values outside of what my culture values, or even what Christian culture values. The pressure to present ourselves a certain way, to spend my time in certain ways, to prove and endlessly labor, is so pervasive.

Create in my family a deep satisfaction in you, not in what we have. Don't let our family reduce following you to prosperity or receiving the life of our dreams or reduce you to a divine waiter. You are our wealth, our portion, our inheritance (Psalm 16:5; Lamentations 3:24). Let us honor you in our times of both plenty and want (Philippians 4:12-13). Unhitch my pride from what we have or don't have, do or don't do.

Reveal ways you would like to set my family free from what chokes us. What is it you want to cut us free from? What idols consume my attention and love, and that of my kids? Give me wisdom to know how to open our grasp.

7

Holy Sexuality

We Are More Than This

When I was little—my parents should be acquitted from this—I took to calling a boy's most private part exactly what it looked like to me. That is, a tail. (I have it on good authority that I am not the only girl to find this a remarkable similarity. Plus, I lived on a farm. Things have tails.)

This generally wasn't an issue until my father, who regularly performs car maintenance, informed the family he was going to fix the neighbor's taillights.

You're seeing this one coming.

Preschool-age Janel: "[Name excluded to protect the innocent] has *lights* on his *tail*?"

This is to say, considering the private nature of sexuality, there's bound to be a lot of confusion, assumptions, and questions, asked or not.

Where do we *want* our kids to get this information?

Parenting kids toward holy sexuality involves a series of conversations to shape their worldview and create open, truthful, shame-free communication.

Permanent Truth

Rather than demonizing sexuality or dividing it into categories of "pure" and "impure," holy sexuality is about

- honoring marriage and God's best design
- targeting a high view of sex based on integrity—a oneness with who we aim to be in Christ
- viewing sex as intimately tied to our wholeness of person
- anchoring our identity in Christ so we're less likely to be swayed by insecurity

(Talking About) Sex Begins in the Kitchen

On my African back porch, a friend's and my own fingers curled around toasty warm mugs of ginger tea that exhaled ribbons of steam. She sort of asked the air around us if it was called rape if a boyfriend forced you. My grip on my mug tightened as her anecdote continued.

But I never talked to my parents about it. They left sex ed to my fifth-grade teacher, and my boyfriend was the one who showed me the rest. My family doesn't talk about that kind of stuff.

I grieved with my friend, recognizing the gravity of what was taken from her.

Later, the situation begged the question: Is there anything on my parental "off-limits conversations" list?

That conversation whispered in my ear when a few weeks later, my then ten-year-old wandered into the kitchen as I decrudified counters and scooped leftovers into waiting Rubbermaid mouths.

"Mom, what's pornography?" An avid reader, he'd come upon the word on the back of a nonfiction work for Christian adults. (This time.) I wrung out the dishrag, tried to wring the freak-out from my face, and reviewed my mental list of How to Deal: What I Believe About Awkward, Hairy Topics with Children.

- I want to be the go-to gal (just as my hubby wants to be the go-to guy) for this stuff with my kids. How I deal with it now affects whether they ask later. It will only get funkier as they get older.

- I want to help them construct their own biblical worldview, assembled not once but piece by piece as we apply each issue to real life, with Scripture informing them, rather than Google or the kids at the back of the bus autofilling the blanks in their minds.

- Evil is not only outside our kids. It's within us because sin is part of us. Therefore, protecting my kids isn't enough. Working with the Holy Spirit, I must shape their consciences.

So...deep breath. Maintain eye contact.

"Great question. Glad you asked. Know how we've talked about sex, how it feels good and welds people together?"

Tripping all over those first sentences, I somehow cobbled together a kid-level definition of porn—and an open warning of its power and addictive properties. I told him it has snared many Christians we know, ruining many marriages. I mentioned billboards and the bodice-busting women on the covers of romance novels on the public library's website. I wanted him to know he has the power and loving obligation to "bounce" his eyes from them.

And I recommended he talk to his dad because dads naturally relate to the male experience—just as I understand more of what Corinne experiences—immediately eliminating the shame factor of speaking with the opposite-sex parent. A bond with a same-sex parent is valuable here. But don't give up if you're a single parent. A college-age female mentor answered a lot of my questions as a teen that felt awkward to ask my parents. Perhaps a youth group or small group leader or a wise relative could step in.

Of course, we should have these conversations privately so our kids aren't perpetually wishing they could burrow beneath the carpet. But questions are an open door to talk about Scripture as we "walk by the way," to the maximum level of what's age appropriate.

Some of the best parents I know aren't necessarily those who withhold information in an attempt to protect their kids. They don't glance around for a fire escape from the awkwardness. They take their child's hand and show them how to navigate difficulty. These conversations secure trust and honesty. They communicate, *I will always tell you the truth. We've got a good thing going here, so come to me with anything.*

Talking to our kids gives them vocabulary to talk maturely about emotions, sticky situations, money, sex, and real life. They're then less likely to be swayed by peers or lies in the midst of their decisions and more likely to know how the Word applies to every situation—and is "useful for teaching, rebuking, correcting and training in righteousness, so that the servant of God may be thoroughly equipped for every good work" (2 Timothy 3:16-17).

Typically, when finding themselves in unfamiliar territory, kids look for indications of where they should turn: "I remember watching something like this." "I don't remember my folks dealing with this." So they're left to their own kid-size toolbox: their best guess, the advice of friends, or other information.

Maybe they'll wing it.

But this is another area where even the most careful, wholehearted, wisely informative training still involves leaving the results up to God. Our kids may make painful sexual decisions—or fall victim to someone else's. Over and over, sexuality is an opportunity to trust and reiterate the power of God's mercy and undeserved kindness to humanity. Sexuality can acknowledge he is always greater than human failure and frailty, a God drawing beauty from ashes.

So stay approachable, occasionally masking your shock or dismay for the sake of welcoming your child as Jesus does.

The Life Stages of the Talk

In our sexually saturated culture, kids are confronted with sex at earlier and earlier ages by media, friends, and billboards. Try to tell your children what they need to know at the earliest appropriate developmental age. Over the years, the more opportunities you take to instill a biblical worldview—and before the topic becomes titillating—the better.

The graphic that follows is a quick reference of the life cycle of the sex talks you may have with your kids. The list following introduces a few more specific topics that are appropriate for each age range. These age ranges are not prescriptive. Every child's development and sensitivities are different, so consider these as you evaluate when to hand each child another piece of the sexual-worldview puzzle.

A healthy sexual worldview is developed from infancy onward. Rather than "the talk" being an event, consider it an ongoing discussion. That worldview is communicated even through how we respond to kids talking about their bodies, how we talk about and to a spouse, and how we refer to subjects like gender: *Women are so...!* or *Gah! Men!* (Do both genders in your house serve one another and communicate worth?)

Your kids are keenly aware of the cues you give off about this "secret" topic. My

Ages 11 to 14
Hygiene
Healthy body image
Tough topics
Personal dating and sexual standards

Ages 8 to 10
Body changes
What the Bible says about sex
How to respond to our culture's views

Ages 4 to 7
The basics: how babies are made and nurtured
God's plan for families and sex is perfect!

Birth to 3
God made families.
He made your body and gender great!

embarrassment, shame, and condemnation—or joy and grace and honesty—can show up when they confront this stuff elsewhere. Even in their marriages.

As parents, we aim to uphold 100 percent of God's holiness and 100 percent of our and his approachability and acceptance amid failure and tsunami levels of shame. If our children experience homosexual temptation or transgender thoughts or get snagged in porn, will they distance themselves and go to elaborate lengths to make sure we never find out? A pastor struggling with same-sex attraction writes, "Christians struggling with SSA often feel especially ashamed and embarrassed...We often feel too dirty to be in community with others, or to be in communion with God."[1]

With your tone and body language, communicate essential truths:

You are a deeply loved child of God. No matter what.

You are also my deeply loved child. No matter what.

You can come to me anytime.

You can trust me to tell you the whole truth.

Your gender is so valuable. Neither gender is better or more valuable.

This isn't something you need to be embarrassed about.

Sex is good and created by God.

Your body and desires are good. Using them the right way is important.

If someone tells you not to tell about this, please trust me; come and tell me.

We're going to hold a high view of sex and your body, with some standards worthy of this gift, but I will not shame you when you mess up.

Sex and Tech

Throughout the life cycle of the talk, take "next steps" to make sure your family is managing technology—and the flow of illicit sex into your home—rather than the other way around. Kids lack an impulse-controlling, fully developed frontal lobe. So that means handing them addictive tech can be like putting a family-size bag of sour cream 'n' onion chips in their lunch box with a sticky note that says, "Careful! Not too much!"

But the problem is far worse with the back-pocket accessibility of porn. The Witherspoon Institute has released an extensive study comparing pornography in its addictiveness to both cocaine and heroin—more like both, since it precipitates the wash of dopamine found in arousal (the same chemical produced by cocaine) and a climax of relaxing release similar to heroin.[2]

These well-trodden neurological pathways widen over time, making them more easily traveled. Because these areas of our brains are particularly changeable, arousal stimuli *carry the capacity to change brain structure,* demanding greater stimulation for the same amount of satisfaction, leading in this case to more twisted forms of porn (for example, physical torture or children becoming linked with arousal). This ultimately results in dissatisfaction with a normal, healthy sexual relationship.

As if that weren't enough, the Institute reports, "There is no timeframe of abstinence that can erase the pornographic 'reels' of images in the brain that can continue to fuel the addictive cycle."[3]

So, along with me, work to stay ahead of technology, and assume your kids are smarter than you think they are. These steps help us control the flow of information into our home. But remember that ultimately, holy sexuality starts in our hearts and continues with open conversation.

- Nix Snapchat, aka "the sexting app." Blogger and youth worker Cameron Cole writes, "We have had many teenage girls confirm that a normal experience for a teenage girl today is for a boy to ask her for naked pictures. We have not had a single girl deny this."[4] Since Snapchat autodeletes photos and videos, kids are more daring about what they post.

- Get a watchdog on your router. We use OpenDNS, a free service, on our router at home. This means that any device using our router is guarded; I choose the level of security. The Circle security device is another great choice.

- No phones in bed at night. All phones are charged away from the bedroom. And create family guidelines asking that all technology be used out in the open.

- Rule: Hand over your phone immediately when asked, or lose your phone. I'm totally that mom performing random checks on my kids' devices. Honestly? My kids' safety and well-being are more important than their privacy. After a friend's child met up with a predator through online gaming, I'm not taking chances.

- Regularly check Internet history and texts. If someone tries to delete something before they hand over their phone, it's mine. You may also enroll in free accountability services like x3watch.com.

- "Last kid in the class to get a phone wins." I appreciated this mantra of a mom in an article about measures Silicon Valley parents are putting in place to guard their kids from what they know well to be the effects of too much screen time.[5] I'm not convinced that my need to communicate with my child always supersedes the dangers they face with a phone in their pocket. We do want our son to be able to handle a smartphone wisely before college, so we opted for an old smartphone, limiting app access.

- Turn off MMS (multimedia texting) to minimize sexting, and turn off data on your child's phone, which hopefully means Internet is accessed largely through filtered routers (school, the library, and home).[6]

- If you have tweens or teens, consider subscribing to Axis's "The Culture Translator," a weekly e-newsletter that informs Christian parents of current trends, along with tips on how to talk about them and have tough conversations.

- Consider a social media contract and phone contract—not from the store but with your teen—to establish agreed-upon guidelines about how your teen will use and not use his or her phone. Include consequences for breaking that contract. Templates are available for free online.

You see the core problem, right? Ultimately, these steps are like attempts to prevent robbery overseas. You can toss up accordion wire, get the best locks, get a dog—the works. But ultimately, if a thief wants to get in—or more accurately, if someone in my home wants to let him in—their heart is the issue.

If our kids can't answer the questions their peers ask—"Why don't your parents let you date?" "Why can't you see that movie?"—standing against the tide becomes a lot harder. So in all our conversations about sexuality, we can hand kids more than a set of rules. We can help them nurture their own convictions through conversations that build on each other.

Talk with kids about:

- boundaries they will choose before they're in a tempting situation

- what kinds of people they hope to date and marry, and what makes a marriage thrive
- family rules, such as no members of the opposite sex in your bedroom or around when parents aren't home, and open doors except when changing, bathing, or using the bathroom
- disease, pregnancy, heartbreak, and the vast, painful fallout of abortion—and how to compassionately understand the tough stories behind these choices (Tip: Don't make this an us-versus-them discussion. If your child is ever on the difficult side of these situations, you want to be an "us.")
- definitions of words (better from you than looking them up)
- how to respond to pressure from someone you respect
- what constitutes abuse, and what to say and do if you're in a potentially abusive situation

One of the best ways to protect our kids is to help them develop thoughtful ownership of their own convictions, motivated primarily by their understanding of God's reward inlaid in holy sexuality. Pastor Kempton Turner explains that when ranchers seek to keep horses on their property, "feasts" are far more effective than fences. When horses are well nourished and enjoying a robust buffet of thick pasture, they're not as tempted by what lies beyond the fence.[7] This falls in line with Hebrews 13:4's reminder for all of us to honor the marriage bed, to show God's plan for the richness and delight it is, rather than just warning our kids to stay away from the fence. (Which is not unlike saying, "Don't press the big red button, kids.")

Sex Can Be More Than This

Surely we can teach and expect our kids to have a higher view of sex because, despite the media's opinion, we are physically able to resist sex. Though it's a valid, genuine need, it's not in the same category as food or air. Consensual, unmarried sex is a bit like consensual shoplifting.

First Thessalonians affirms this higher view of sex: "It is God's will that you should be sanctified: that you should avoid sexual immorality; that each of you should learn to control your own body in a way that is holy and honorable, not in passionate lust like the pagans, who do not know God; and that in this matter *no one should wrong or take advantage of a brother or sister*" (4:3-6, emphasis added).

There's a reason this holy sexuality chapter is after the self-control and fasting chapters. Holy sexuality is about controlling our bodies for the sake of a sweeter, more loving, more mind-blowing beauty of unselfish, monogamous sex that re-affirms our marriage vows.

God continues in 1 Thessalonians with gale-force words about the critical nature of sexual integrity, using words we shy away from: "The Lord will punish all those who commit such sins, as we told you and warned you before. For God did not call us to be impure, but to live a holy life. Therefore, anyone who rejects this instruction does not reject a human being but God, the very God who gives you his Holy Spirit" (verses 6-8).

But the church itself is reeling from some of its own nomenclature. Some of us grew up amid "purity culture," which created two categories of people: pure and impure. But as sinful beings, none of us fall in the *pure* category. Ephesians 2:8-9 speaks of a salvation "not from yourselves." Implying we fall in a different, more favored class of Christian defames this vital aspect of the gospel.

In her work, Dr. Juli Slattery instead argues for the term sexual *integrity*, implying a wholeness of substance, an undividedness. Our behavior can increasingly, year after year, match who we claim to be because of Jesus. That means sexual integrity continues into marriage—where couples pursue healing from past sexual hurts, turn away from porn, and work against selfish married sex.[8]

For millennia there have been people who were able to wait—who possessed the moral fiber, self-control, respect of others, regard of their own sacred sexuality, a high bar for marriage (see Hebrews 13:4), and the power of God to say no for a little while longer. And they've humbly sought forgiveness and restoration when they've selfishly taken from someone. Remind your kids that their desires and struggles aren't unique to them or their generation—and that they have the power to make these sacred decisions too.

I resonate with historian Lauren Winner, who writes poignantly, "The biblical story of the body is very different from the stories *Cosmo* and *Maxim* tell. The magazines (and movies, TV shows, and advertising campaigns) speak of bodies that are both too important and not important at all. Scripture speaks of bodies that God created in His image, bodies that are doing both redemptive work and being redeemed."[9]

Good guys, like the biblical Joseph, run the other way. And call me naive or an upended ostrich, but we can ask our kids for more. They thrive when we beckon them to more than what the media make of them. (Scientific research backs me up on this: "Impulsivity is a tendency with adolescence, not an absolute."[10])

A Note to My Kids: We Are Whole People

I was a good Christian kid, raised in the church and lathered in vital discussions of sexuality, peer pressure, and well-considered dating standards. Those were critical in shaping me toward steadfastness and sexual faithfulness.

Yet inwardly (and well within the range of normal), I longed so much for approval, for validation of who I was. Insecurity led to flirtatiousness and gaps I longed to have occupied by guys. Remember those soul holes discussed in chapter 1? When kids are flailing for who they are, their identity could undermine all our desires for their sexual integrity.

If my kids read this someday, I'd want to tell them, *You are capable of being a giver far more than a taker.*

You were made for so much more than intimate theft, even if it's accepted as the norm. You are capable of waiting to give and take something this holy until you can give someone your whole life, rather than stealing part of them for yourself and refusing to care for the rest.

I know you'll hear something diametrically different from nearly all of your world. But know you can't compartmentalize your sexuality or someone else's body. We are whole people.

I believe you can stand among people of integrity, and that, by God's grace, you will.

Writing on the Wall: Practical Ideas

Here are more detailed conversation starters, separated by age groups. (Again, these age ranges are guidelines. Please consider your child's particular development and temptations.)

Birth to 3

- God loves us. Everything he makes is great!
- God made families and marriage to give us a picture of his love.
- He made boys and girls each special. They have different body parts. Here is what they're called. (Studies show that using proper terminology helps protect kids from abuse.)
- Your genitals are special and private. They feel good to touch, but we don't touch them in public.
- Your genitals shouldn't be touched by anyone except Mom or Dad or a doctor—like when you're taking a bath, using the bathroom, or being examined by a doctor. If someone touches you, it's okay to say no and run away. Tell your mom or dad if someone tries to disobey this rule.

Ages 4 to 7

- You can talk with me or your other parent about this stuff. But let other kids' parents be the ones to talk to them.
- God made boys' and girls' bodies different. I'm glad God made you the way you are! Boys and girls both need to be strong, intelligent, compassionate, nurturing, and hardworking.
- Remember, no one except your mom or dad or a doctor should touch your genitals. Tell your mom or dad if someone tries to disobey this rule.
- Here is what happens in a mother's womb as babies grow. Here's how babies are born and fed.

- God originally designed for families to have a dad and a mom, and for them to have kids after they get married. Not all families look like this. But we treat everyone with love and kindness. Let other kids' parents be the ones to talk to them if their families look different than you expect.

- Here are the basics of how babies are made—people often call this "having sex."

- God made sex for married people. When a man and a woman feel attracted to each other, their bodies can lie very close together. The man's penis becomes hard and straight, and it can fit in the woman's vagina. The man and woman move their bodies together, and at the end, sperm from the man's body is left in the woman's body, where it can join a tiny egg from her body. That sometimes makes a baby, which grows inside the woman's body. Sex can feel very good and makes the husband and wife feel close. But this is also a private gift, which a couple enjoys alone, maybe when they don't have clothes on. So you can ask your parents questions, but please don't talk about this with anyone else or make jokes about it. Let's respect this special gift.

- What we watch on TV or play on screens affects our brains, so we watch what builds up our brains and hearts, not what tears them down. We should spend most of our time doing things in the real world, with real people.

Ages 8 to 10

- God designed sex only for heterosexual marriage. He created sex as a way to create babies, as a gift for closeness and unity in marriage, and as a "glue" to make a man and woman one flesh. Marriage between a man and a woman shows the world what God is like and Christ's relationship with the church (Mark 10:6-9; Ephesians 5:22-33).

- Here's what the Bible says about sex. (Use passages like Genesis 2:24-25; John 8:1-11; 1 Corinthians 6:12-20; Ephesians 5:3; Hebrews 13:4;

1 John 1:9; and verses from the Song of Solomon to openly communicate God's design for pleasure.)

- The Bible says homosexuality is a sin (Romans 1:26-28; 1 Timothy 1:9-11; Leviticus 20:13). But even as we oppose sin, we love homosexuals like any other sinners, like we love ourselves (check out Matthew 22:27-29 and John 8:1-12). We treat all people, no matter their sin struggles, with dignity and respect (1 Peter 3:15), counting others more significant than ourselves (Philippians 2:3). And you need to understand the delicate, inflammatory nature of discussing this matter with people outside our family. Homosexuals are nearly five times more likely to attempt suicide, so our compassion is critical.[11]

- Here's how your body will change and how the bodies of the opposite sex will change.

- Here's how you can react to pressures from the outside world about sex—and some ideas of what you can say, using strong, calm body language, looking the person in the eye without making excuses or apologies: *I don't want to. I'm not "everybody." If you loved me, you wouldn't pressure me to do something I'm saying no to. If we need to have sex to stay together, then we need to break up.*[12]

- Here's what it looks like to dress and behave appropriately. No, you're not responsible for how the other gender behaves. But we approach modesty and behavior—flirting included—with an attitude of being our "brother's [or sister's] keeper." (In contrast to Cain, Jesus is the ultimate brother's keeper, who rescued the rest of God's family—see Hebrews 2:11-15). We also consider verses like 1 Corinthians 8:9: "Be careful...that the exercise of your rights does not become a stumbling block to the weak." Christians will interpret modesty and behavior differently from their secular peers.

- You need to know the proper names of your body parts so we can communicate clearly. Please let me know if someone makes you uncomfortable or touches a part of you usually covered by your swimsuit! (Note: Other parts can be touched inappropriately, but start here.)

- Let's practice saying "stop" to someone if you don't want someone to touch you. And if someone says they want you to stop, you need to respond too.

- Let's talk about who you trust; keep me posted if you no longer trust someone. Even safe people can suddenly make you feel unsafe. So trust your instincts and draw boundaries when it comes to someone who makes you feel uncomfortable.

- I want you to know I'll always tell you the truth about sex—and I'll believe you when you talk to me too.

Ages 11 to 14

- Let's talk about healthy body image and avoiding some of the traps into which our culture often falls.

- Here's how your body (and mind and emotions) will continue to change. Let's talk about the details you might be tempted to look up but which I'd like to explain to you instead so you don't stumble upon raunchy explanations.

- Here's how your body will change as it develops—and the basics of what the opposite sex is also juggling.

- Let's talk specifics of how a woman gets pregnant and delivers a baby.

- Here are a few terms you may hear that you'll need to understand referring to sexual acts and our bodies. Some of them will be vulgar—usually because they're degrading rather than holding sex and a person's body in high value. But I want you to know what people are talking about so you don't joke about it the wrong way, or Google it (which could lead to things you can't unsee), or be naive. The Bible says it's "shameful even to mention what the disobedient do in secret" (Ephesians 5:12), so I won't go into full detail or tell you everything you might hear someday. Please ask me if you hear about something and don't know what it is.

- We need to talk about the gravity of pornography, and we need to talk about masturbation. (Seriously. Don't let your kids find out about this one from friends in the locker room.)

- Here's why God made sex for marriage and never outside of it. Let's begin to set your personal dating standards: what kind of person to date, when to date, and physical activity in which you won't engage. Remember that forming an alliance with someone who isn't a Christ-follower is like trying to hold hands with someone when you're on two moving sidewalks heading in opposite directions (see 2 Corinthians 6:14-15).

- Let's continue to talk about what the Bible says about homosexuality and how to respond with love and truth.

- Boys and girls bear mutual responsibility for keeping themselves and each other from lust (that is, illicit sexual desire) and taking every thought captive to make it obedient to Christ (2 Corinthians 10:5). Furthermore, girls aren't the only "brakes" on a physical relationship. Let's protect each other.

- Particularly for girls, the first few times—perhaps longer—can be painful and unfulfilling, particularly when the relationship isn't committed. Find out more about why 83 percent of women prefer committed sex.[13]

- Many people feel deep regret when they sin sexually. But you might not immediately. It might feel satisfying and very connecting. Yet that temporary pleasure could have lifelong consequences and undermine your married sexual relationship. But God will love you no matter what. I will love you no matter what. I will not shame you. And no sin is too much for God to forgive. Come to me when you're struggling with something, and we'll work through it together.

For more activity ideas, discussion questions, and other resources for teaching sexuality, visit janelbreitenstein.com/permanentmarkers/sexuality.

Fresh Ink: Resources for Vibrant Faith

- Kristen Jenson's *Good Pictures, Bad Pictures: Porn-Proofing Today's Young Kids* is a helpful, emotionally intelligent, secular resource to talk to older elementary and younger middle school kids about the realities of porn and how it affects our brains. There's also *Good Pictures, Bad Pictures Jr.: A Simple Plan to Protect Young Minds* for younger elementary kids.

- You might also like Kimberly and Zack King's *I Said No! A Kid-to-Kid Guide to Keeping Private Parts Private.*

- I like Justin and Lindsey Holcomb's *God Made All of Me: A Book to Help Children Protect Their Bodies* (New Growth Press, 2015). It's a great picture book to start conversations about our bodies—and keeping them safe—in constructive ways that celebrate God's creation.

- To start the conversation of appreciating kids' gender at a picture-book age, try Marty Machowski's *God Made Boys and Girls: Helping Children Understand the Gift of Gender.*

- We also found helpful Stan and Brenna Jones's classic *The Story of Me* and *Before I Was Born.*

- Teens may dig the YouTube channel *Paul and Morgan*—a series of Christian advice vids on life, love, and dating.

True Colors: Discussion Questions for Kids

- From what we've talked about, what's more beautiful and loving about married sex that outshines the temporary high of doing what feels good? Why is waiting for married sex the better choice in the long run?

- What are some of the not-a-good-idea things people are trying to get you to do at school? Which ones are the hardest to say no to? Why is it so hard? After this discussion, let's go have some fun, and remember: You're more than what your friends think!

Think Ink: Contemplative Questions for Parents

- Who was influential in shaping your views of sexuality? How did they speak of or demonstrate those values?

- What current circumstances feed into your views of sexuality? (Hint: If you think you're not influenced, that's problematic.)

- What are your fears in talking to your kids about sex? (Tip: Get honest about them so they don't subconsciously manipulate you.)

- What pain and regrets do you carry about your sexuality?

- In what ways might you personally lack "sexual integrity"—a wholeness in the way you pursue God-honoring, unifying sexuality?

- If a Christian friend of yours struggled with sexual urges or sins outside the norm, would you be able to respond compassionately the same way God responds to your temptations (see 1 John 2:8-11)? Would your friend see in you God's acceptance of them—totally apart from what they do?

- Do you believe Jesus's work on the cross is as powerful to embrace homosexuals, those who've undergone abortions, transgender people, etc. as it is to embrace you?

Even in marriage, it's our hope to move ever closer to God's idea of sex: an expression of each-for-the-other unity. Sex carries the unique quality of acting as a microcosm of our lives and eventually a marriage, of how we relate and love. That's why preparing our kids for God-honoring, whole-person sexuality (or even lifelong chastity in singleness) starts so young. We're saying, *Here. Love like this.*

Prayer of the Dependent Parent

Lord, the voice of my culture is so loud when it comes to sex. It's hard to know what, when, and how to control so my child knows how to respond with strength, dignity, honesty, class, and integrity to all temptation's avatars.

I ask for your protection of my child and their heart when I'm not there. Let my child get caught as soon as possible if they're dabbling in sexual sin.

It's so easy for my fears in parenting to loom larger than your power and loving sovereignty over my kids' lives. Bring me to deep trust in you regarding my kids' deepest, most intimate vulnerabilities. Draw me to surrender even here. Even in my parenting nightmares, you create resurrection and beauty from ashes (Isaiah 61:3). Ultimately, I'm only your manager of these kids—your kids. Remind me again that my success or failure here is not the goal; it is not the sign of my worth as a parent.

Forgive me for the ways I haven't acted with sexual integrity. Show me ways my sexuality diverts from the wholeness you created me for.

Help me be a safe emotional place for my child and their failures or wounds; let me replay your redemption of me, your inexhaustible grace, over and over.

8

Community

Almost Home

A friend of mine recently moved into a new house—on the same weekend her husband surprised her with a new puppy and her adult kids came home for her birthday. Her adult foster son's toddler was padding around as I popped in the door. We sat at the dinner table surrounded by tilting stacks of boxes.

Know what I love? She brought out a plastic bin of granola bars for lunch, with a side of some tubs of applesauce and a jar of peanut butter. I 100 percent meant it when I told her how much I loved that our friendship had hit the granola-bars-and-a-spoonful-of-peanut-butter level.

Our authentic conversation nourished my soul. Her hospitality welcomed me into her reality—considering me more important than her image. Classy meals and lipstick aren't why we stick around each other.

I've found that people who visit our house may not remember whether I put out a clean hand towel or they stepped on a toy. But they remember if I was truly, undistractedly present with them. They remember if I was interested in their lives—and whether they felt loved.

Permanent Truth

Community is about:

- choosing interdependence with the full diversity of Christ's body, rather than dysfunctional isolation
- helping others feel "at home," even when meeting them on the street—allowing them to glimpse God's open arms and intentional care
- receiving others and being received with emotional presence and safety
- caring relentlessly and practically amid the daily stuff of life

I continue to think my friendships as a whole benefit from more fingerprints and less mascara or neckties. A little more spruced-up appearance leaves us that much more isolated because, as John Lynch and his coauthors reflect, "No one told me that when I wear a mask, only my mask receives love."[1] Presenting artifice to others prevents them from loving our true self beneath.

The Disease of Isolation

In his book *Lost Connections,* Johann Hari relates how, for decades, social scientists have been asking people a simple question: How many people in your life could you call in a time of crisis? In the 1970s, the most common answer was three. Today's most common answer?

Zero.[2]

Hari explained that in their brain scans, lonely people tended to spot threats twice as quickly as socially connected people. The lonely were hypervigilant, more likely to take offense, and more suspicious of others. Hari continues, "It was only a long time into talking with these social scientists that I realized every one of the social and psychological causes of depression and anxiety they have discovered has something in common. They are all forms of disconnection."[3]

Isolation lies contrary to our God, who has lived in perfect community for eternity within the Trinity, and who took daily walks with his image bearers in a garden. Who defeats the isolating power of shame.

To be clear: I'm not talking about being electronically connected or even about social media connectedness, both of which *increase* kids' tendency toward depression and anxiety.

I'm talking community.

Some people might say, "Community. That's kind of like a Facebook group, right?"

Well, no.

Community is about relationships that love relentlessly and practically—through depression or a miscarriage or the career that evaporated. Through seasons where one party might give or pursue more than the other. Or seasons with as many melty beads on the floor as dirty dishes on the counter.

We aim to train our kids to acknowledge our unvarnished need for each other because, as Christians, isolation is dysfunctional. As the apostle Paul reminds us in 1 Corinthians 12, the interconnectedness of the body of Christ is vital: "The eye cannot say to the hand, 'I don't need you!'" (verse 21).

What If Friendships Are the One Choice We Have?

The need for community hits me like a tennis shoe between the eyes because in some of the scariest and darkest times of my life, I've found myself shutting down and shutting out. Isolation honestly felt safer than needing others, than exposing myself to judgment or rejection or misunderstanding. (If we do this, do our kids get the idea we should *pretend* friendship?)

Sometimes the effort toward friendship feels herculean. I've even been guilty of offering just enough of an appearance of authenticity—a "curated imperfection." What if our facades and efforts to keep it all together or appear need-free contribute to our own implosion? With all the uncontrollable factors in our lives, what if defeating isolation is the one choice we do have in staying healthy?

A year ago, in a cancer scare with our son Will, the gravitas of the situation and the precious nature of my grief seemed to settle themselves on my lips. In a season of dire stress, I didn't feel I could risk someone misunderstanding the sacredness of my grief—the private intricacies and particular, searing losses. But I often associate my needs with considerable shame, so asking for help felt like adding a stone atop the boulder grinding my face into the ground. But John kept telling me, "We want to walk this road in community."

When I don't think I need others, when I choose aloneness because I think I'm better off or safer being independent, I choose against God's design of a whole body.

One of Jesus's final prayers for his people before his death envisioned a radical opposite of cultural isolation: "I pray...that all of them may be one, Father, just as you are in me and I am in you. May they also be in us so that the world may believe that you have sent me" (John 17:20-21).

Becoming one requires our presence. Authors John and Stasi Eldredge note, "The gift of presence is a rare and beautiful gift. To come—unguarded, undistracted—and be fully present, fully engaged with whoever we are with at that moment. When we offer our unguarded presence, we live like Jesus."[4] Returning from Uganda, I was stricken that people now seemed so hungry for someone to listen to them. We feel a deep longing for people to share our stories with, depend on, and feel known by. As a culture, we are slowly starving. And on this trajectory, our kids are headed for a future even more isolated.

In Genesis 2:25, God sets an ideal of marriage that is *naked and unashamed*. If community is in concentric circles, with marriage being one of those most intimate circles in the center, isn't there an element of our relationships that longs to be naked-faced, naked-hearted, just-as-I-am...and finally be unashamed? Finally be accepted as we are, embarrassing needs and all? Dependent, and okay with that?

So what if we lived differently? More vulnerably? More—dare I say—intrusively?

Training Kids to Be a Safe Place

I'm channeling my inner Fred Rogers here. Part of what draws us into community is the ability to trust and depend on each other. Mr. Rogers is famous for telling kids to "look for the helpers."

Can kids grow into helpers too? Absolutely. Adults should still bear the mantle of being the primary helpers. But we can help kids mature into community members who receive others and their pain.

A friend of ours was recently diagnosed with cancer, so our kids brainstormed ideas for being good, safe friends. We talked about the stages of grief, listening without interrupting, and what not to say—including platitudes like "It's God's will" or "I understand" or "Everything's going to be okay."

Community is far more than interdependence. It's a need for us and our kids to have at least one emotionally safe place, one emotional "home." John and I have frequently prayed for one trustworthy, quality friend for each of our kids. At times, having or lacking that friend has defined a season for them.

Author Drew Hunter asserts that churches often encourage community but forget friendship—ostensibly "because friendship is exclusive, particular, and preferential, while the call to Christian love is all-inclusive." But the truth is,

> deep community is most likely a place in which each person goes deep with a handful of others. These are not isolated cliques (us four and no more) but overlapping networks of relationships.
>
> ...Greater love [*agape*] has no one than this, that someone lay down his life for his *friends*" (John 15:13 ESV, emphasis added)! According to Jesus, no love exceeds friendship love...Far from being at odds with Christian love, friendship is a central way in which we live it out.[5]

So, as you seek community for your family, start with a few core, unashamed relationships.

And get un-alone.

Writing on the Wall: Practical Ideas

Build a web of connections.

Grab a ball of yarn and stand with your family in a circle (this activity can involve family friends too). The yarn-holder keeps hold of their piece of yarn, tosses the yarn to someone, and says that person's name along with something unique and valuable about what they contribute to your family. This continues several times, building a web demonstrating how interconnected you are.[6]

Share love with neighbors and friends.

Buy a coffee or bake or buy some goodies. (Even guys can bring someone their favorite drink, right?) A friend regularly muffin-bombs my house (you know who you are). When she and her kids make a treat, they make extra and share the love with neighbors and friends.

Muffins have a way of making the world feel smaller.

Teach your kids to greet well—the first brush with hospitality.

Try walking through the following steps with your kids. Pretend an imaginary rope is traveling up your back, up through your head to the ceiling, helping you to look the adult in the eye. Hold the person's hand like it's a baseball you don't want to drop—firmly, but not a death grip. And know the six magic words: "Hi! I'm _____. How are you?" (You can leave out your name if you already know the person.) Most adults can take it from here.

Give pointers for time around the table with a guest.

No electronic devices, phones included. Help them to have a few (open-ended) questions prepared for the guest. (You might suggest a few things going on in your guest's life.) Ask the kids to listen—without interrupting. Suggest silently counting to two before chiming in. Practice manners beforehand, and give everyone a small role in preparing; even little kids can lay out spoons.

Coach kids to act as host.

When there's a new kid at school or church, encourage your kids to introduce and help the newcomer know what the conversation's about. They might have a question in their back pocket ("I'm into drawing. What about you?").

Have kids make a dish or a whole meal.

During the summer, my kids take turns cooking for our family. They slowly adapt to the administrative aspects of hospitality (Ingredients! Timing!).

Host a Bring-Your-Own-Meat grill night.

Rotisserie chickens. Potluck at the park. Compostable plates. "Breaking bread" with others—that is, sharing a meal—is held in high priority in the Bible (see Acts 2:42). But it's a dying art form because the work can feel overwhelming! Our own image management is often what stands between us and the community we need and long for. How can you dress down hosting to still form this critical community-making skill in your kids? Together, focus on relational warmth and ease—as Jesus welcomed us—rather than your family's ability to impress or have your act together.

Pray for other voices in your kids' lives.

These are people abundant in areas where I sorely lack and intimately involved enough to speak into my kids' lives. Ask someone to mentor your child. Capitalize on a mutual hobby, like the guy from church who takes my son to the shooting range or helps another son with archery. Or, if your child is struggling, ask a kind adult friend to take them out for coffee to simply listen. Before a birthday, ask people in your child's network to send e-mails for you to print out, read aloud, and save.

Model asking others for help in areas of weakness or need.

This can include picking paint colors, gardening, knowing where to take the car for that weird noise. When your child wants to learn something, help them think about others in the community they could ask.

Teach the gift of presence.

Community is about being fully, undistractedly there. You can do this by putting down that load of laundry (or, hello, your phone) when kids are talking to you. Model giving the people in front of you priority, and save texting, browsing, and social media for alone time. If you show them how, it'll be easier to remind kids to be headphone-free when they're with company, to look people in the eyes, and to ask others questions about their lives.

Dads model community too.

If moms primarily model a skill, there's a chance kids will get the idea that it is only for women. Dads, you have a killer role in modeling vulnerability and need for others—true, interdependent masculinity. Bring your kids along, when appropriate, to activities with your friends: Ultimate Frisbee, disc golf, skiing, game night, coaching, or camping.

Remember, social media is not community.

No one should broadcast their most intimate feelings where there's no one to look them in the eyes, ask questions, and receive them. Nudge your kids into face-to-face relationships with safe friends.

Go behind the scenes.

When your kids talk about another child's problems, help them peek behind the scenes at what could be going on in that child's life. What are they feeling? What might their world be like at home? (My eyes were opened when I found out years later that a "mean girl" in my life had been undergoing her parents' divorce.)

Help your kids move beyond insecurity in relationships.

Teach them to look beneath their own words or actions to the heart attitudes beneath: "Why do you think you wanted to make him feel that way?" Don't praise appearances only (shy away from phrases like "people will think you're..."). And encourage them to be an authentic iteration of themselves in every group of people.

Encourage your kids to be a safe place.

Help them look out for other kids—on the playground, at the lunch table, and anywhere else some kids might feel isolated, rejected, or fearful. Help your kids understand what it means to be a "safe place": People feel they can come to us and be real and be accepted, not rejected. We listen first, without the need to fix. People aren't like puzzles, waiting for us to plug in the right piece of advice or information.

Teach reflective listening skills.

Explain that people of all ages first need to tell their story, to be heard. Then kids can ask questions and respond with good listening skills, like looking the speaker in the eye, not interrupting, and nodding and making small noises ("Uh-huh!" "Wow!" "Oh man!") to show they're listening. They can also repeat back a little of what they heard—"So, how did you feel when he said...?"

Let the person know what they're feeling is okay. I tell my kids that feelings are like dashboard lights in a car: They're not wrong, but they tell us what's going on under the hood. In fact, sometimes emotion tells us what logic may not have figured out yet. It's what we *do* about them that is right or wrong. So kids can say, "I think it's okay that you feel that way."

Increase your borders.

Intentionally welcome people of all socioeconomic backgrounds and races. Ask your kids if they can think of someone who seems different from them whom they want to get to know better. Invite that person to "break bread," just as Jesus ate with all kinds of people.

Put kids in charge of cooking.

On summer evenings, I put kids in charge of cooking our family's evening meals. It trains kids in the administrative aspects of welcoming and gathering others: planning what to cook and how much, balancing a meal (no, we can't have mashed potatoes, rice, and bread), and getting all the dishes ready at the same time. Even better, help your kids form a collection of their favorite recipes.

Build a network.

Whom can kids contact when they have a need—both kids and adults? Whom can they help and pray for in return? Consider relatives, friends, Sunday school teachers, and babysitters. When your kids need help, brainstorm together about whom they can talk to. Conversely, if a friend is in need, get intentional about how you can help. Pray for them. Bring them a meal. Offer for you and your kids to babysit. Help your kids mentally build a structure of people who mutually depend on one another. You may want to help your kids assemble this network visually. Find a printable version of a "People I Can Count On" poster to post on the fridge or in a cupboard at janelbreitenstein.com/permanentmarkers /community.

For more activity ideas, discussion questions, and other resources for teaching community, visit janelbreitenstein.com/permanentmarkers/community.

Fresh Ink: Resources for Vibrant Faith

- Check out some children's books that show the power and navigation of community. I like:

  - *Stone Soup* by Jon Muth
  - *An Apple Pie for Dinner* by Susan VanHecke and Carol Baicker-McKee
  - *Wilfrid Gordon McDonald Partridge* by Mem Fox
  - *I Really Like Slop!* (An Elephant and Piggie Book) by Mo Willems
  - *A Sick Day for Amos McGee* by Philip C. Stead and Erin E. Stead
  - *A Chair for My Mother* by Vera B. Williams
  - *What a Hat!* by Holly Keller

- Food allergies (different from sensitivities or preferences—and life-threatening) can make hospitality a scary reality for families. But they're an increasing reality for so many of us! Some will prefer to bring their own food to keep family members safe. Grab tips for welcoming these often-isolated families at janelbreitenstein.com/permanentmarkers/community. You'll also find ideas for simple dishes to make hosting easier.

True Colors: Discussion Questions for Kids

- Which friends help you feel like you can be yourself? What ideas do you have for making a friend feel like they can be themselves?
- What makes someone a great listener?
- Are there friends who make you feel like you have to hold back a bit because they might make fun of you or not understand?
- Who makes you feel most at home and welcome, like you belong? Whom do you think you could trust and tell anything?

- How could we make people feel truly comfortable in our house?

Think Ink: Contemplative Questions for Parents

- What's the next step you'll take to be more vulnerable and connected with someone?

- What most stands in the way of you being emotionally "present" with others? These might be physical obstacles (a harried schedule, fatigue, your phone) or emotional barriers (failure to allow ourselves to be loved and received by God and others).

- Think about the friendships that have most shaped you. How have they changed your life for better or worse?

- What fears or barriers stand in the way of your hosting with your whole heart? (Sometimes it's not the right season. When we had young kids, it was survival season. But the idea is to make sure it's only a season.)

- We tend to think more activities connect us more with people. But what if the quantity of your activities sucks the quality from your relationships? What's one activity you could say no to for the sake of being more present with others?

I'm fascinated by Jesus's expression that, to the rest of the world, what sets us apart as his followers is how we love each other (John 13:35). As a family, rather than community stuffing itself into the cracks of our lives and schedules like necessary spackle, I hope it's part of the frame holding all of life together.

Prayer of the Dependent Parent

Lord, so much is working to pull us apart from other people—not the least of which is my own frenzy and my own fear. Help me model dependence and community rather than image management. Anchor my sense of worth in what Jesus has done, rather than in my own sense of perfection. Bring my family out of isolation and hurry, and lead us toward unity and full presence with others, like you were present with us (John 1:14).

Set in front of us the community of Acts 2:

> They devoted themselves to the apostles' teaching and to fellowship, to the breaking of bread and to prayer. Everyone was filled with awe at the many wonders and signs performed by the apostles. All the believers were together and had everything in common. They sold property and possessions to give to anyone who had need. Every day they continued to meet together in the temple courts. They broke bread in their homes and ate together with glad and sincere hearts, praising God and enjoying the favor of all the people. And the Lord added to their number daily those who were being saved (verses 42-47).

9

Discernment

Sorting the Skittles

S ay you're walking down the street as a family. There on the sidewalk, a couple you don't know erupts in an argument at full volume. She's a Mount St. Helens of vile obscenities and venomous accusations. He shoves and vehemently threatens her. Someone they know comes out to successfully intervene, but your kids' eyes volley questions faster than a Star Wars blaster. What do you do?

A. Cover your kids' eyes with your free hands and shoot the couple the evil eye as you stalk off. ("Some people! Get your act together, folks.")

B. Smile at the couple. Act like nothing happened.

C. Wait until you're out of earshot, then mumble, "*Whoa*. What a jerk. And what a witch! How does he live with her? If I ever see you kids acting like that..."

D. Something else?

Permanent Truth

Discernment is to interact with God throughout the day in soul-level listening to his Spirit—creating ownership of our faith in an intimate, personal relationship. It is about:

- learning to apply the Bible to daily situations

- picking out various rights and wrongs, personal reactions, and amoral behaviors—like sorting a bag of Skittles by color—rather than making sweeping, all-or-nothing statements

- listening for God's voice and watching how he works—and looking for opportunities to participate with him

Kids present or not, we joust with these situations daily: a teenager mouthing off to his mom in Starbucks, the friend who gossips at our dinner table, the language on primetime TV. We're caught: Part of us wants to push back at such behavior. Part of us wants to offer the benefit of the doubt.

We wrestle with what values look like considering full measures of compassion and mercy and justice. Lately, we're encouraged to keep our own "version" of truth and values to ourselves: *Your values are A-OK as long as they don't interfere with mine.*

Rich possibility lies in choosing to discern right from wrong. On my better days, running into someone else's wrong is a chance to play out all over again to someone else the kindness God shows me constantly. That kindness is the air I breathe.

You know people who exude this kindness. They lean in. They make you want to slide down your inner mask and examine what's really going on under there.

In the context of a loving relationship, discernment extends a chance to gently, precisely apply healing to what embezzles life and true comfort from a person and those they love, with as little damage as possible.

I think of it like a fellow athlete throwing an arm around a shoulder: *We're in the game together. Try this.*

Our hearts are dark, and they're complex places. As Aleksandr Solzhenitsyn so poignantly wrote,

> If only it were all so simple! If only there were evil people somewhere insidiously committing evil deeds, and it were necessary only to separate them from the rest of us and destroy them. But the line dividing good and evil cuts through the heart of every human being. And who is willing to destroy a piece of his own heart?[1]

Determining whether someone else's actions are right or wrong is important. But if we poorly manage our responses, if we convey arrogance and lack of nuance and understanding, our behavior can fall short of genuine love and even holiness. What's the difference between humbly, firmly identifying what's right (even if only in our own minds), and bulldozing people?

In a couple of words: humility and love. In John 8, where a woman caught in adultery is brought to Jesus, the Pharisees believe they finally have the ammo needed to trap him: "In the Law Moses commanded us to stone such women. Now what do you say?" they ask him in verse 5.

Jesus's response is simple. "Let any one of you who is without sin be the first to throw a stone at her" (verse 7).

The men wander away, oldest first (perhaps more aware of their own collected failures). When no one is left to kill the woman, Jesus says, "Neither do I condemn you…Go now and leave your life of sin" (verse 11).

This entire narrative forms an essential model for us and our kids. Rather than an opportunity to peer down from a moral high horse, discernment is a chance to lay down the stone we were about to lob. Judgment, in this story, kills. Mercy hews out space for a restored life.

Deuteronomy 6 does say we must talk about God's commands as they lay their loving grid over all of life—on the road, in our home, when we lie down, when we rise. And maturity has its "powers of discernment trained by constant practice to distinguish good from evil" (Hebrews 5:14 esv). Discernment is like looking for infection beneath a microscope, with the goal of eliminating what infects us.

Yet when we're about to slide others' faults under the scope, discernment also whispers, "What do you have that you did not receive? And if you did receive it, why do you boast as though you did not?" (1 Corinthians 4:7).

There's more than a little Pharisee inflating all our chests. We feel it in that subtle inclination to utilize someone's weakness to quietly acknowledge ourselves as making better choices, possessing better character. Or we view a certain type of people with mild disdain. Or we mentally rehearse a friend's inadequacies. Not long ago, I was ashamed to realize I'd been selectively comparing myself to others to make myself feel good as a parent.

The opposite of judgment, I'm convinced, is the gospel. It's keeping my own need for effusive mercy in front of my eyes, extending that same gospel to others from my daily experience at the cross. *This* is wise discernment for our kids.

So one possible solution to the previous dilemma could be…

D. When you're alone as a family, ask your kids questions about what they noticed, your concern for the couple evident in your tone. Ask what they would do if someone treated them like that. Acknowledge what you don't know about the couple and what they might be going through. Pray together for the people you saw.

I've created the following table to help me slice between judgment and discernment. I wish I'd known this—making it part of me—before I'd left such a trail of ashes among people I care about. Maybe it will help you avoid similar destructive mistakes. I now long for the scent of Christ I leave with people—from the bank teller to my ten-year-old—to be that of compassionate truth-telling and graciousness. Training my kids in discernment means identifying what's right in light of all contributing circumstances, responding a lot like the way Jesus came to us: alongside (rather than above) in both grace and truth (John 1:14).

Judgment	Discernment
self-serving	loving; operates from a place of humility; speaks at the proper time and in the proper way (Ephesians 4:29)
works to curse and punish	works for deep, lasting goodness
separates; creates "us/them" categories	creates unity, removing the sin in our way and remembering we're all equal at the cross
condemns	offers hope; bears the burden together
looks at the outside; does not seek to see oneself in the person's situation	acknowledges what we don't know; seeks to compassionately understand
wields shame	takes its cues from grace
sees people without hope and faith in view	sees people as being "in process," with capacity to change
makes self superior	works not from above, but diligently alongside (Galatians 6:1-2; Luke 18:13); keeps our own utter and constant struggle with sin in mind
often focused on outward behavior	works prayerfully with the Holy Spirit to understand the whole truth in someone's heart, asking God to first work change within oneself (Matthew 7:5)
often operates out of fear, pride, or control	beckons into the light, as God's kindness leads to repentance (Romans 2:4)

Flight of the (Media) Navigator

Am I the only one who cringes at the media evaluator role of parenthood? I constantly feel like the bad cop, monitoring the Xbox and Microsoft reports and Fall Out Boy lyrics.

Here's what I don't want to happen: I don't want my kids to get to college and not know how to evaluate the media everyone's gulping down like Kool-Aid—or hole up with their Jesus music and flip out when someone plays Imagine Dragons. I know God gives all of us different perspectives to raise our own kids. I'm personally trying to navigate going outside my preferred "bubble boy" mode while still shooting for "unstained from the world" (James 1:27 ESV). The method I'm working through with my kids is training wheels for a biblical worldview rather than not doing stuff simply because "Mom said no."

So if my kids want to purchase a song, I first have them look up the lyrics for me. We discuss what people are craving in this song. What's it about? What do they want? Is anything in this song not meeting those desires in ways God says are okay? Are there ways that their solutions overpromise, like expecting romantic love to solve all our problems?

I also ask my kids how Jesus is the ultimate yes to all these desires. In every love song, every song about dreams or passion, how does God ultimately fulfill those real cravings?

Conclusions our kids come to themselves are 100 percent more effective than those we come to for them. (No, that's not an actual statistic.) If we can have open conversations about what they think is right or wrong, steering them in the right direction with good questions, we raise kids who can choose right for themselves.

So walk with your kids through their media—not just to say yes or no, and not even to be the bad cop. We're helping our kids construct a worldview about what kind of entertainment they'll marinate in and helping them build wise judgment for more complex issues they'll inevitably encounter.

Perhaps the most critical discipline in discernment is knowing God's Word. I think of a basic analogy: If my son were away from home and wondered what he should do about something, he would probably know what to do based on what he's heard me say before. Similarly, kids have 66 books of God's Word to help them hear God's voice and learn and absorb exactly what he's said. Over time, they gain discernment based on what they know of God and his ways.

To help them in this process, let's ask thoughtful questions about how they listen to God; that is, allow the Holy Spirit to apply God's Word to their situation. Let's probe their hearts, encouraging them toward a genuine relationship with God.

In conversation, we can quietly work toward helping kids understand more than meets the eye. Move toward thoughtful, detailed complexity so that the pieces of each situation are accurately weighed: As Proverbs 4:7 puts it, "Though it cost all you have, get understanding." Ask kids for relevant verses that apply to situations you encounter, add your own, and together pray verses over your world and those you love.

Writing on the Wall: Practical Ideas

Allow me to suggest a few ideas from a season where I'm personally discerning popcorn kernels from Airsoft bullets on my kitchen floor. Grab a few ways to work smarter, not harder, in trust-filled and Godward ways.

Read Hebrews 5:14 and have a blindfolded taste test.

Can kids tell the difference between peanut butter and almond butter? Honey and maple syrup? Salt and sugar? Almond milk and cow's milk? Cheerios and Honey Nut Cheerios? Ketchup and tomato paste? How can they tell? Answer: They've tasted enough of at least one in each pair to know the difference between that and a "fake." Discuss how we discern good from evil by constant practice.

Have one partner stand at one end of your living room and blindfold her. If you have an odd number in your family, the extra person can be a referee and official distracter. Toss obstacles of pillows or cushions onto the floor. When you say go, the voices of the unblindfolded partners should guide the blindfolded partners across the living room—without touching any obstacles. It gets hairy with all partners yelling at once—especially if you have a distracter shouting nonsense.

Talk to your kids about the need to pick out the Holy Spirit's voice amid all the other voices in our lives—particularly that of Satan, who "masquerades as an angel of light" (2 Corinthians 11:14) and "prowls around like a roaring lion looking for someone to devour" (1 Peter 5:8).

Chat about the sermon on the way home from church.

Keep a general climate of goodwill toward the church (rather than downright pickiness). Acts speaks of the Bereans, who were of "more noble character" because they "received the message with great eagerness and examined the Scriptures every day to see if what Paul said was true" (17:11). What do your kids agree with? What do they have questions about or disagree with?

Sort the Skittles.

Open a small bag of Skittles, M&M's, Smarties, or another multicolored candy. Ask kids to sort them into colors. (Smarties will require more careful examination and better lighting!) Challenge kids: "Are you sure this one's green? How can you tell? It looks a little like the yellow in some ways. What colors are mixed together to create this color?" Talk about discernment—the need to sort through a situation and determine what's wrong, what's right, and what's neither or a mix of both.

Find some popular memes.

In its humor, what is each meme trying to say? How would the Bible agree or disagree with its message? Hint: Often it's not all bad or all good. For example, the meme might be telling the truth about something that's frustrating, but complaining rather than addressing it in a constructive way.

Ask, "How could it have ended?"

Choose a media headline, movie, or historical event, and ask how it could have ended had a person involved exercised discernment. Do this without judging or acting superior; it's an opportunity for some lighthearted humor. What could have happened if a main character (maybe Shakespeare's Juliet?) were able to phone their past self and say, "You might not want to do that"?

*When talking through tough issues, ask kids to
physically place themselves on a spectrum.*

Maybe the "spectrum" is from one end of the living room or sofa to the other. Where do they fall if one end of the room is "not confident" and the other end is "very confident"? Where do they fall if one end of the room is "pro welfare" and the other end is "against welfare in all circumstances"? In an encouraging environment, ask them to present their reasoning, using Scripture when possible. The goal isn't to get your kids to think like you; it is to exercise scriptural discernment and progress in their reasoning skills.

Help older kids examine what they're reading.

When Corinne read *Lord of the Flies*, I asked her what the author was trying to say. We delved into a great discussion of humanity without social constraints, how humans decide on whom to bestow authority, and what she thought would happen if her English class were suddenly stranded on a desert island. ("Yikes, Mom.")

At the risk of oversimplifying, I've noodled on a method kids can use on their fingers to think spiritually about decisions. Hey! There's even an acronym: **G**ertie **H**ad **L**unch **W**ith **T**om, examining the categories of God, Heart, Love, Wisdom, and Trust. Grab a printable version of this at janelbreitenstein.com/permanentmarkers.

WHAT DOES HIS WORD SAY? HAVE I PRAYED ABOUT THIS? **GOD**

WHAT DO I WANT AND FEEL—BOTH GOOD AND BAD? IS SIN KEEPING ME FROM SEEING CLEARLY? **HEART**

WHAT WOULD IT LOOK LIKE TO THINK ABOUT OTHER PEOPLE AS MUCH AS I'M CONCERNED ABOUT MY OWN PROBLEMS? **LOVE**

WHAT DO GODWARD THOUGHTFULNESS, GOOD JUDGMENT, AND EXPERIENCE SAY I SHOULD DO? **WISDOM**

WHAT WOULD IT LOOK LIKE TO DEPEND ON GOD? **TRUST**

For more activity ideas, discussion questions, and other resources for teaching discernment, visit janelbreitenstein.com/permanentmarkers/discernment.

Fresh Ink: Resources for Vibrant Faith

- The children's book *A Bargain for Frances* by Russell and Lillian Hoban is a fantastic resource to start the conversation about manipulation in kids' friendships.

- We've enjoyed the *Sticky Situations* series (Tyndale, 2001, 2006) to help elementary-aged kids think through concrete ethical situations they might encounter.

- PluggedIn.com, Kids-in-mind.com, and CommonSenseMedia.org help parents preview media before their kids dive in. When my kids wanted to try out Star Wars'® *The Mandalorian*, Common Sense had great conversation prompts: "Why do you think George Lucas and Disney decided to make a Star Wars TV series? Characters who die are mostly faceless characters, often in uniform. How does that change your perception of the violence? How do the characters in *The Mandalorian* demonstrate courage and compassion?"[2] My daughter has since come back to me with more thoughts about facelessness and violence.

- ClipShout—at clipshout.com/fcce—offers a two-week free subscription on their library of licensed movie clips for (secular) character education!

True Colors: Discussion Questions for Kids

- When you're trying to decide what's right, how do you know what God wants you to do?

- How can you tell the difference between what God wants you to do and what you want to do?

- What book have you loved that had an ugly cover or maybe had something spilled on it, got moldy, or smells weird? What about the opposite—a book that looked good but ended up being trash? How can we be too easily swayed by something's appearance? Have you found this to be true with people or other things?

Think Ink: Contemplative Questions for Parents

- When teaching your kids discernment, what are your natural inclinations? Are you likely to lean toward judgment? A lack of confidence or hatred for evil (Romans 12:9)? Favoring emotion or gut instinct over Scripture? Smothering emotion or intuition entirely?

- What are you most likely to mistake for the Holy Spirit (intuition, convenience, ambition, my own idols, pride, or what others want me to do)? What tends to stand in the way of your discernment?

- What spiritual practices or circumstances help you shut out the "noise" around you and allow Scripture and the knowledge of God to inform your decisions?

The skill of spelling requires a number of aptitudes: forming a letter with your hands, photographic memory, working memory, phonological understanding, sound-letter associations, and more.

Teaching our kids discernment combines a lot of aptitudes too: memory of and understanding of God's Word; empathy; higher-level abstract reasoning, which develops later in the human brain; humility and self-restraint as we wait for more pieces to the puzzle we're assembling; cultural awareness; and a lot more. So keep in mind that your kids' discernment is cumulative, constantly growing like a ball of Play-Doh as life experiences are added, processed (accurately, we hope), and observed.

Prayer of the Dependent Parent

Lord, thank you that your Spirit is far stronger and more accurate than if I were my kids' conscience! I'm grateful you go with them wherever they go.

Please teach my kids' hearts in ways they can't resist, and bring them to surrender to you in every corner of their souls. Let them know and love your ways. You say your sheep know your voice (John 10:3-5,27); let my children know and follow yours.

In their discernment of good and evil—down to the lines of good and evil in their own hearts—let them encounter how deep and wide your undeserved favor is because of Jesus.

10

Service

Downward Mobility

We traipsed down the street in Kampala, Uganda—a motley crew in flip-flops, water bottles banging against our legs. Jack, always the wild card, was the one whose hand I needed to hold. Motorcycle taxis purred past us with odd cargo: butter-colored jerry cans, loaves of bread piled around the driver, live chickens hanging by their feet from the handles like creepy bouquets.

Once we turned the corner, pavement dissolved into streets of dust. The air was crowded with smells of charcoal stoves, smog, and something fried. Children ran in clothes with broad holes, the milky soles of their feet flashing. We knew we were getting close when we saw the goat who seemed endlessly, enormously pregnant.

Astoundingly patient South Koreans had converted The Giving Tree from a storefront to a neighborhood library—but one where the books stayed put. Maybe it seems contradictory that the books couldn't be checked out, but in a neighborhood unfamiliar with the luxury of a library, allowing books to be checked out would mean the disappearance of these books shipped from around the world. So children clustered on the cement floor, guiding their fingers beneath the words or flipping through vivid illustrations. Adults trickled in for literacy and computer classes.

On Thursdays, my children held a library story time. We would sing and act out Sunday school songs my kids had picked out. Then each of my children old enough to read would fluidly narrate books toted from America to Uganda: *The Berenstain Bears; Frog and Toad*, a repeated favorite; *Harold and the Purple Crayon*. Then my kids would assist as the other children huddled over their lime-green tables for a craft, usually while some diaperless toddlers hauled in by an older sibling ate the crayons and peed on the concrete floor.

What I loved: There is something beautiful about kids learning to wash someone's feet, so to speak. Jesus paints swaths of a kingdom where the greatest among us is the servant (Matthew 23:11), not the smartest, strongest, skinniest, most attractive, most charismatic, or most athletic. A kingdom where God, when he was among us, wrapped a towel around his waist and gently scrubbed manure from his people's toenails. *Have this mindset*, Philippians says.

Service trains our eyes to see the neighbor in our path—like the Good Samaritan (Luke 10:25-37)—and not step around him but deliberately, sacrificially move toward him.

Selective Service

Years after that trip to the library, when the heavy, cloudy reality settled on me that we would likely move back to the States, I wasn't sure how I would translate "service" to an American context for my kids. No self-respecting library was likely to let ten-year-olds run a story time—and that wasn't needed.

So I prayed that God would somehow draw an arrowed line for our kids from service in Africa to service here. Strangely, it worked.

Was it because I'd asked? Because our eyes were sweeping for opportunities? I can't tell you. A Fall Fest was hosted for the community by a local church. The Salvation Army needed bell ringers. (Gosh, that was frigid. But shoppers even brought my kids bags of M&M's from inside.) A family next door, with the father

Permanent Truth

We look for opportunities for humble, happy service everywhere. Service pries our fingers from our own agenda and primes our hearts for "Here am I! Send me!" It is

- ideally beginning with an inward transformation of loving someone (though our hearts can admittedly follow action)
- being content without reward, recognition, or paybacks
- not always being compelled by emotion, but faithfulness
- a lifestyle

deployed, had a daughter with Down syndrome and a near magnetic attraction to my younger kids.

I'm cautious now, as I see the ways my home culture loves achievement and hurry and image, and that service carries the danger of *more to do* when we're trying to share dinner together. So, as with the rest of life, our family attempts to say the right no so we can get to the right yes.

Sometimes that means service is less of an event and more of a lifestyle, like caring for the elderly couple that needs their drive shoveled. It also means we look at the ways our kids are naturally made. *This one likes helping with the soundboard at church. This one's fantastic with kids. This one could be a greeter when the church doors open.*

Deciding where to serve can be tricky, particularly in a way that's sustainable, rather than a big flare of energy that peters out. What can you do to serve members of your own family? Then, expanding your "circle," how can you serve your school, community, or church?

Talk with your kids to discover causes they're passionate about, and help them design an activity they could do: hosting a baby clothing drive for the pregnancy center, cooking relief meals for parents doing foster care, finding a missionary kid pen pal, or playing a pickup game of basketball with a kid whose parents are in the middle of a divorce.

Your child's imagination and your resources are the limits. Serving transforms your home into an aircraft carrier as its members are fine-tuned, then deployed into the neighborhood.

How Much Do I Push?

My kids often loved reading the stories and singing the songs at our African story time. But the novelty waned after the first few weeks. And, of course, other kids dumped out my kids' water bottles or acted obnoxiously.

This required some discernment as I watched for signs of when to push for the sake of perseverance and love, when to ease up for the sake of protecting my kids' hearts from bitterness and joylessness, and how to add to the "carrot" (the reward).

My kids took turns having a week off, and we always went for *kasooli*—roasted maize—afterward. We strategized together about the ornery kids. And at the end of my kids' service, the sponsor of the library honored them. It was like a perfect dessert making you think that the meal wasn't half bad. But if the situation had persisted, I would have been okay with ferreting out a more gratifying way to serve.

Sacrifice, faithfulness, and perseverance are unmissable lessons. And I would love, when possible, for service to mean a lifetime of swelling, burbling joy, tugging them toward God rather than away. But I also hope my kids become adults who know when it's okay to let go. Hopefully, they listen to their bodies and emotions and trust that God will have someone to take over—or not—if they need to say no.

I attempt to handsomely reward my kids when they serve and give them healthy breaks. I love when they look forward to service and when they volunteer for it, when we laugh together and get a smear of mud on a cheek.

Yes, service is its own reward! Yet, we also want to associate serving with pleasure. God inlaid his own reward system in us, washing our bodies' systems with endorphins when we love on others. And he promises rewards in the future too. So plan a movie night after your time of serving, and consider kids' service as their chore for the day.

When Loving You Is Really About Loving Me

Martin Luther King Jr. once remarked, "A man may be self-centered in his self-denial and self-righteous in his self-sacrifice. His generosity may feed his ego, and his piety may feed his pride. So without love, benevolence becomes egotism, and martyrdom becomes spiritual pride."[1]

We've all seen our kids (and ourselves) serve in ways that really aren't about the person being served; they're about our feeling superior or needed or holy. (We've probably been on the other end of that too.) Humble service begins with seeing ourselves as laterally needy to those we help, as the rescued because of Jesus. But sometimes it is hard to know when we're being self-righteous and when we're being authentic.

I've vamped a bit on Richard Foster's contrast between self-righteous service and true service.[2] Perhaps the chart can help you interpret your motives and aim for authentic service.

Self-righteous Service	Authentic Service
prefers the big, sparkly jobs	finds it almost impossible to differentiate the small from the large
calculates results and expects gratitude and compensation	finds happiness in service itself
picks and chooses whom to serve, mostly because of image	is indifferent to an audience; almost never notices when others watch
is blown around by moods and impulses	gives steadfastly because there is a need
is short-lived	is an ongoing lifestyle
puts others in their debt; builds self up as the giver, breaking community	builds community; is subtle and unpretentious, putting no one under obligation
needs to know people see and appreciate the effort (with proper religious modesty, of course)	is fine with hiddenness; doesn't shy away from or look for praise

Writing on the Wall: Practical Ideas

Considering your current mission may just involve getting your kids to eat peas with a fork, what could authentic service look like? Your energy and capacity aren't endless. Pick a couple of ideas that dovetail with your family's subculture, your circumstances, and your community.

Hold an egg demonstration.

Try this spin on an activity from author Jamie Miller. Place an egg in a glass filled with 1 cup of water. Have ¼ cup salt nearby and a tablespoon. As the egg sinks, explain to kids that this is like a person having a hard time. (Who can they think of who's struggling right now?) Kids take turns adding a tablespoon of salt and, with each addition, suggest a kind act of encouragement. Watch as the egg is "held up" by kindness. Read 1 Thessalonians 5:11 together: "Encourage one another and build each other up." Explain that when people are at their lowest, they often need to be compassionately lifted up by the ways we serve them.

For family devotions, consider a foot-washing ceremony.

After one of your kids reads John 13:12-17, focus on its final message: "Now that you know these things, you will be blessed if you do them." Seeds Family Worship has a song for this verse so you can memorize it together. Then talk about whether your kids feel like it really is better to give than receive—but acknowledge we all need to do both.

Don't confine kids' service at home to chores.

When my kids were still waddling around in diapers, I watched a preteen hop up and immediately help his mom with a younger sibling. I thought, *I want kids who will respond to service whenever they're asked.*

Occasionally, ask your kids to pick up what's not theirs (hello—like their parents are doing).

It's good for them to learn to be their brother's keeper (Genesis 4:9), cleaning up after someone else, as Jesus did for us. Rather than shielding your kids from dinner duty or carrying in groceries, frequently request their assistance. It won't all be fireworks, but help them get excited about making someone's favorite dish, or have a contest to see who can hit the hamper with their sibling's dirty clothes. You're training them to be the chief servant in their own homes someday.

Challenge your kids to secret service.

My youngest son, Jack, felt frustrated this year when kids were rewarded for helping others at school, but no one saw him when he was helpful. Though I love rewards, they work against serving in secret (Matthew 6:2-4). So, challenge your kids to three "secret services" a day. They don't have to tell you what they did but can give you a "code word" for each mission they accomplished.

Create a group of people who serve together.

Corinne and some friends created an open group of girls who serve, pray, and hang out together. They even designed their own T-shirts! Could your family partner with another or cart along some friends to serve together, then have a game night afterward?

Ask your kids to serve in situations where they might otherwise be takers.

They might help at grandparents' houses, pick up others' plates after a meal, or look for ways to help a teacher. In general, it's good to "leave a place better than you found it."

Make a hot fudge pudding cake to illustrate service.

Memorize Mark 9:35 together: "Anyone who wants to be first must be the very last, and the servant of all." Together, make a hot fudge pudding cake.* Talk about how God's kingdom is upside down from the way the world does things. The best is on the bottom because "anyone who wants to be first must be last." Ask kids what the world values in its leaders: power, beauty, popularity, achievement, wealth, ease, superiority. But what did God's leader and example, Jesus, do differently?

Talk about everyday situations that provide openings to serve.

Remind kids that the heart of a servant is about how we show up in the world. Though some of the following ideas could act as one-offs, we hope to communicate that service isn't a project; it's a way of being and of seeing the world.

Talk about everyday situations that provide openings to serve.

- Sit with that kid in the cafeteria who's alone. When a public restroom has paper towels all over the floor, pick them up with a clean paper towel.
- Let someone in a hurry go ahead of you in line at the grocery store.
- Stay after an event to help clean up.
- Bring coffee or donuts to construction workers in your neighborhood.

---

* If you haven't tried this before, check out the recipe at cafedelites.com/hot-fudge-chocolate-pudding-cake.

- Make a no-sew fleece blanket for the friend who's in the hospital or could use something to cuddle during a loss.

- Babysit as a family for a date night for a young couple, a single mom, or a family plowing through a rough patch.

- Visit a nursing home or adult day care center. You could play bingo, lead a sing-along, or bring board games, nail polish, and lotion to rub hands or feet.

- Shovel snow, rake leaves, or mow the lawn for a neighbor. Or when they're gone, volunteer to water plants or care for a pet.

- Pick up trash in your neighborhood.

- Tutor a younger child after school or play with one who might need extra love.

- Write notes to people who could use a little affirmation or encourage- ment (e-mail works in a pinch).

- When a sibling is having a bad day, put your heads together to make a plan to encourage them.

- Prepare a care package for a missionary or someone who is sick. E-mail ahead of time to see what small items they'd love—maybe chocolate chips, a book your kids loved, beef jerky, or a small pack of Legos. Include notes from your kids. Pray together for the recipient.

- Adopt a family (without making them feel like a project): Pray and talk together about a family who could use some extra love. What will your strategy be? What are their true needs (as opposed to what you guess they might want), and how can you help them in a sustainable way?

Fresh Ink: Resources for Vibrant Faith

- Focus on the Family's KidsOfIntegrity.com has innovative ideas for devotions, object lessons, and service-oriented action. To drive this life skill home, visit their Generosity page.[3]

- I love the picture books below that teach compassion—for that flow of inward transformation to outward action. In reading, kids encounter stories outside their own experience—equipping them for when life imitates art (and certainly making that real world less scary).

  How Many Days to America? by Eve Bunting

  Say Something! by Peggy Moss and Lea Lyon

  Smoky Night by Eve Bunting

  Mufaro's Beautiful Daughters by John Steptoe

  Listen to the Wind by Greg Mortenson

  The Lady in the Box by Ann McGovern

- And these chapter books make for compassion-inducing read-alouds:

  Wonder and *Auggie & Me* by R.J. Palacio

  El Deafo by CeCe Bell

  Out of My Mind by Sharon M. Draper

  A Long Walk to Water by Linda Sue Park

  You Were Made to Make a Difference by Max and Jenna Lucado

  Rules by Cynthia Lord

- Look for opportunities in kids' movies to talk about compassion too— like the messages in *How to Train Your Dragon*

- At janelbreitenstein.com/permanentmarkers/service, find ideas for kids to work with organizations that are already making a difference, 40 ideas to raise globally-minded kids, and links on creating care packages for the homeless.

True Colors: Discussion Questions for Kids

- Why do you think Jesus washed his disciples' feet? Isn't that kind of gross? Why would God want to serve us in ways that seem gross?

- How did Jesus serve us?

- Who serves you? How do they serve you?

Think Ink: Contemplative Questions for Parents

- When you think about service, how do you feel? Inspired? Overwhelmed? Guilty? Exhausted? Resentful (for ways you've served resulting in burnout or other negative experiences)?

- What do you want to pass on to your kids from your own experiences in service? What do you want to improve or avoid?

- Service takes time and emotional energy. Is there anything you could cut out to create this space so you're not more exhausted and can serve from hearts that actually want to?

- In what areas do you struggle most with selfishness? What's one step you could take to loosen your hold on what's "yours"?

When I think of a God who models love through stripping and kneeling to wash the dirty feet of his creatures and submitting himself to their capital punishment, I remember service grows on the tree of humility. To paraphrase C.S. Lewis, God knows our pretenses and posturing interfere with any quality relationship, hindering our ability to truly love.[4]

Service ideally follows humility, but the two flow in a circle after each other. Only God can produce that kind of meekness in my kids. But service is one way to cultivate toward that end.

Prayer of the Dependent Parent

Lord, thank you for serving us, ultimately, in the cross—starting from the minute you stepped into our mess among a bunch of animals and their smells, far from what was flashy or convenient or honored in this world. We know what love is because you laid down your life for us (1 John 3:16).

I can't create a service mindset in my family. We were born into selfishness. Our natural inclination is to look after our own needs.

Make us a family of servants for your honor, not ours. Show us our attitudes that exalt us even in our serving. Let giving be our daily lifestyle, and help us make space for it so we're not more frenzied and burned out.

Remind us we're not what we do for you. We're not more worthy because of what we do. Let our serving bubble up from the way you've filled us and served us—from the ways we've received your overwhelming love. Give us your eyes—your compassion—to see what others around us are carrying, and to care about it.

11

Sharing Our Faith

Loving Them This Much

It was on vacation, walking to a train, that our family met "Gretchen." Conversation unfolded among us in the blistering sunshine. We were all drawn in by the details of her home country, the stories of her life there. At 30, Gretchen was pretty and successful. She traveled around the world.

Perhaps that's why I was intrigued by two of my kids after disembarking the train, when she'd warmly wished us well and waved to us out the window. Separately, they asked me if we could pray for her, that she'd know Jesus too.

I could be wrong about my kids' motivation at that point. But I think they wanted something more for Gretchen, whose life seemed—even to an attentive child—as if she were chasing something.

We've all seen evangelism's insurance policy equivalent, or even been its recipients: the tract left with the woefully small tip or in the bathroom stall. The door-to-door "training." The scalding lecture about the consequences of our current lifestyle.

Compare these with the blind man who can't wait to tell people, *Hey, I*

Permanent Truth

Sharing our faith is about:

- a courageous compulsion, emerging from God's love for us and our mutual love for others, to tell of God's change inside us—a contagious joy.

- caring enough to compassionately seek out where a person most feels their own longing for God, including their questions, story, and pain.

- as Ruth Haley Barton puts it, "an invitation to spiritual transformation offered by someone who can bear witness to that transformation in their own life...so much more than selling an insurance policy regarding life in the hereafter."[1]

can see! When our own encounters with God have cooled or been a disappointment, our evangelism is inevitably less convincing or motivated.

To put it simply, sharing with people the faith that's given me so much life has to flow directly from loving God and loving them. If I slide my agenda before my concern—*We must get this person saved from hellfire and brimstone!*—I'm the annoying gong, the clanging cymbal, the car alarm everyone wishes would shut up. People don't hear, "God loves me!" They think, *You didn't even respect me enough to really see me.*

Not Your Grandma's Evangelism

I noticed a similar phenomenon after living in Africa. Often we Westerners give—quite generously and sacrificially—because it makes us feel good to finally do something. And in all senses, we should.

But at times, we give in a way that cements Africans in handicapping cycles of poverty. When we don't take time to understand the nuances of their need, we sometimes put our own desires (to assuage our guilt, to feel happy about giving, to help, etc.) above their needs.

Decades ago, East Africa had a thriving textile industry. But once Westerners began sending their charitable used clothing, the industry tanked and has nearly vanished. Now, East Africans walk around in castoffs we often can't sell in our own nations because of the clothes' condition.[2] Eager efforts to "help Africa" robbed them of what they did have to propel themselves forward, leaving them the poorer for it.

Similarly, when our evangelism is agenda-driven rather than thoughtful, rather than love- and people-driven, our delivery methods of the gospel can become a point of (yes) anger and resistance to those in front of us.

Great evangelism techniques shouldn't help us better manipulate people toward knowing Jesus. They should help us love and tell the truth better.

I do believe there has been a vast generational shift in how our culture is reached with the mind-blowing message of grace and true peace. Though there was unquestionably a time for tracts, formulas, giant events, and the evangelistic equivalent of a "cold call"—and many people are still reached this way—those techniques can trigger knee-jerk repulsion, as younger generations consider faith a starkly personal issue. These techniques can even stoke the fires for future flat-out rejections.

In its demand that we acknowledge our utter need for God and our helplessness to save ourselves, the gospel is offensive enough. First Corinthians 1:23 calls it "a stumbling block to Jews and foolishness to Gentiles." We don't need to add to the offense with insensitive social skills.

That doesn't mean I shouldn't talk to the woman next to me on the flight or express on Instagram something God has done. That sensitivity to social situations doesn't dampen my courage or the frequency with which I diligently work to extend this gift. It means that in this culture where people can sniff out an agenda a mile away, my boldness and sense of urgency must proceed solely from deep regard for the person in front of me. Like in parenting my kids, all agendas for them must proceed from that source.

When I was trained as staff with Cru, president Steve Douglass taught, "The gospel flows best through the holes in people's lives." We are most receptive to Jesus in the seasons and areas where we most feel a need for his answers, where we ache with longing for God and an eternal home. (Keep in mind all those people who sought out Jesus because their own healing propelled them.)

We see this in Acts 17 as Paul approaches a group of Stoic and Epicurean philosophers in Athens's Areopagus. He begins with affirming their own spiritual searching and locates one of their longings—expressed to the point of worship via an idol "to an unknown god." Yet, then he logically appeals to a point of their misunderstanding: "The God who made the world…does not live in temples built by human hands" (verse 24).

Before they even have a chance to get their feathers ruffled, Paul returns to another point of agreement, using a poet from each group, both Stoics and Epicureans, connecting with the philosophies of both and their natural curiosities. He's clearly engaged with current cultural ideas.

So, talk with older kids about how to compassionately listen to and come alongside friends in hard times with true hope and comfort, using even song lyrics or what they've seen on Hulu. (See the section in chapter 8, "Community," for ideas for helping kids be a safe place.)

From the Barna Group's research, President David Kinnaman reports that non-Christians' hopes in discussing religion are, first, someone who *listens without judgment*—followed by *not forcing a conclusion.* However, only one-third see this in Christians they know personally![3] So, we can train kids to patiently hear someone's story and ask intricate questions core to who they are. To accept in faith that helping explore and lift someone's shame takes longer than a seven-minute conversation. To discuss our kids' own mess or unanswered questions. (Non-Christians are sometimes better at this.)

A lot of our kids want to please and fit in. They can leverage this to be winsome in how they share Jesus—and yet, confident despite inevitable rejection, and even, as we are warned, persecution (2 Timothy 3:12).

Wrath Is Real

One of my ongoing confusions is my children's inability to unpack their lunch boxes. (I refuse to do this on principle.) Isn't it better to do it in the premold phase? But on a Monday morning, I saw Baden unpacking said lunch box. Actually, he was placing the leftovers packed *the previous Friday morning* back into the fridge. No food wasted, right?

Color me revolted.

Like the inevitable furry petri dish soon to make itself known in my Rubbermaid, God's wrath is coming because of sin, even though we can't see it. And to pretend we are not sinners in the hands of an angry God is dangerous. Condemnable.

God's words to Ezekiel also caused me to shudder: "If the watchman sees the sword coming and does not blow the trumpet, so that the people are not warned, and the sword comes and takes any one of them, that person is taken away in his iniquity, but his blood I will require at the watchman's hand" (Ezekiel 33:6 ESV). In this verse, I understand there's a grave responsibility on me for those I "watch over" to adequately communicate God's warning of what's coming.

If I love someone, it doesn't make sense not to care enough to share Christ with them—it would be like hiding the cure for cancer. Atheist Penn Jillette agrees:

How much do you have to hate somebody to not proselytize? How much do you have to hate somebody to believe everlasting life is possible and not tell them that? I mean, if I believed beyond the shadow of a doubt that a truck was coming at you, and you didn't believe that truck was bearing down on you, there is a certain point where I would tackle you. And this is more important than that.[4]

We ask our kids to confess sin not just because it is good for their character. We model confession because God is indeed holy. His wrath is indeed real.

Thankfully, Jesus has taken every ounce of God's wrath for us and for our kids, if in fact they choose him as their substitute. In Romans 8:1, the apostle Paul promises that there is "no condemnation for those who are in Christ Jesus." We need not be fear-driven parents who make more of sin than what Jesus has done for it! But sin isn't a naughty kitten who needs to be put outside. It is a cancer. And it separates us from God. True care propels us to let people, even strangers, know the fullness that has finally satisfied us, finally filled all the holes in our souls.

How could this unfold with real kids like mine? (I'm talking about a child who, upon request, sucked on his brother's eyeball to the point of leaving a hickey. But I digress.)

The Place of Apologetics

Apologetics unquestionably serves its place in the church in proving the veracity of our faith to many who would turn away amid loud voices defying Christianity's historic and scientific plausibility. Apologetics also preserves our kids.

Yet, rather than *arguing* someone to Christ in stratifying or scoffing arguments, which can occasionally cause a person's heels to dig in even further, you can make sure these conversations take place in ways that affirm someone's intellectual curiosity and journey. Intellectual arguments can be channels for questions the heart asks: questions of human pain and darkness, of whether we really can love God with all our minds.

Yet our kids could have all the right answers, but none of the heart to hear and love the person in front of them. If kids see an unbeliever as an opponent rather than a person with deep questions, they will answer what a person's heart isn't asking. But if they see a non-Christian or a questioning Christian as a person feeling their way toward God (Acts 17:27), perhaps they can view the situation more like finding a dangerously injured, even combative person lost in the woods, who desperately needs someone to stop, shoulder the pain, and help them to the trail.

Any child—any human, for that matter—naturally wants to share what's fantastic in his or her life: "Look what we found in the clearance aisle!" "I met someone!" "I got into my top choice!" So, before sharing our faith comes the experience that our faith is compelling and life-changing and worth sharing. Kids excited and filled by Jesus will share their faith as a natural outpouring of who they are. To give a reason for the hope they have (1 Peter 3:15), first they must have that living hope.

This is one of the areas where they pick up cues from us. Ours is not a dogged religion that "works our way to heaven." It's an experience of acceptance and purpose from a stunning, captivating God. As we experience him, our kids are equipped every day to know what their faith looks like in any given situation.

As much as tracts and other tools can give kids brilliant steps and thus boldness to share their faith, I am increasingly convinced that traditional methods can actually distance people from our kids because the methods are socially alienating to a modern Western audience. Day after day, the best and truest evangelism seems to be accomplished by *great lovers of people and lovers of God*. A lack of evangelism—a horizontal issue—may be an indicator of a vertical problem: a lack of a lively, leafy relationship with God. The vital message for our kids: We are not the savior, but the saved. We're about humility, not results.

Writing on the Wall: Practical Ideas

Make your home the locus.

Did you know that much of the evangelism in the book of Acts happened from homes?

In the past, I was always coached to invite people to church—and this is still a fine idea. But the nuanced cultures of churches can, depending on the person, occasionally cause our friends to feel like outsiders. We're not inviting them to a social club with all the trimmings or seeking to pass the evangelistic buck to a trained professional.

Instead, we can invite kids into a place where they see everyday love, maybe alongside a plate of cookies. One of the best evangelistic tools around is a healthy home with an open door and a little extra time.

Yet, this insight should not instantly transform your chaos into Stepford mode: a plate of warm cookies on the counter, no one arguing, zero snark. I don't believe that veneer is appealing to the general public because that's what it is: a veneer. The message of the cross isn't "Fake it better, and with feeling!"

Jesus doesn't make us perfect. He makes us forgiven. Hopeful. Lovers of grace. And those, when lived inward, then outward, make for a compelling home.

Expect a wild card.

For holidays, or dinner together, or a weekly open-invitation soup-night, or a simple after-school hangout, ask God to open your home to whomever he would have you invite. With both sides of my family, I can expect guests who might not have a lot of extended family or who need a place to hang out. They're welcomed like family, and maybe even have a gift under the tree. I don't always know whom my own kids will bring home, but that's a happy part of our home being God's.

Articulate your faith.

For weeks around the dinner table or while driving, we'd quiz our elementary-age kids: *What's grace? How is someone saved?* We'd ask application questions too. Help them understand and love how God has saved us inside and out, not with confusing platitudes—"I asked Jesus into my heart!"—but in kid language—"I said yes to Jesus paying for my sins." "I couldn't get to God because of my sin. But God sent Jesus to me."

Help your kids learn to tell their story in various lengths. Talk with them as they write down ideas about life *during* and *after* meeting Jesus—as well as *before*, if that's something your child can remember or that helps better communicate Jesus's transformation.

Pray regularly as a family for those around you to know Jesus.

A couple of years ago, Corinne started praying for the salvation of an important adult in her life. We had some good conversations about how she might gently make her faith known to him.

As we prayed for him, God also seemed to give us opportunities to care for this person amid his family's hard times. Soon, Corinne asked me about more overt ways to talk with him about Jesus. She was only in fifth grade, but her lack of guile, I think, made it less awkward than if she were an adult. She crafted him a special Valentine: "We love because he first loved us" (1 John 4:19).

As a family of fellow sinners, let your prayers for your community voice true love and humility and that God is the great softener of hearts. After all, he softened ours! Ask him to help you make the most of every opportunity (Ephesians 5:16) and to season your conversations with salt (Colossians 4:6).

Role play.

In this chapter I've shied away from handing you methods that might help you articulate your faith or approach someone better, but possibly cause you to love them worse. In our current culture, it may prove more helpful to guide our kids into creating and guiding *spiritual conversations.* A lot of our effective training with our kids comes in coaching them through situations with kids at school and ways to help their friends. Corinne consistently chews over girl drama with us—how to respond with love to the girl who snubs her, how to tactfully help the left-out kid. (See how these are the message of Jesus, worked out?) Jack needed help handling a bully, so we prayed for the bully, as well as about ways to return a blessing for an insult (1 Peter 3:9), which is, in a form, the gospel played out.

I find evangelism to be more like service in this respect: We may not share Jesus with everyone in our path. But like with the Good Samaritan, sometimes it's about meaningfully helping the one in our path.

Older kids might like having a few questions
in their back pockets to help them.

Here are some they could use after hearing about something tough going on in a friend's life.[5]

- Would it be okay (or totally awkward) if I prayed for you right now?

- How has [what happened in your life] shaped how you think about God and spiritual stuff? Who do you lean on when you're freaking out? Where do you go when you're stressed out?

- What's the story behind your tattoo? (I kid you not. It's a great way to hear about a transforming moment or something meaningful to the bearer.)

- What's the biggest question that's been rolling around in your head lately? What do you believe about Jesus? (The Bible? Life after death? Truth? Suffering?)

Important: Help your kids know when to drop the conversation, particularly when people aren't interested or things get offensive or heated. Anger indicators include crossed arms, raised voices, clipped sentences, jabbing gestures, continued failure to engage, or people directly saying, "I don't want to talk about it." Your child could respond with, "Okay. I can respect that. If I've frustrated you, I hope you'll forgive me."

Talk about your own pain.

When Will weathered a cancer scare, God used his faith brightly—*not* because my son had an agenda to use his pain to win his friends, but because as he worked through his pain, he talked about his trust in God no matter what would happen. Because our culture seems to have a Spidey-sense about anything *manufactured* (not to discount intentionality), speaking naturally about what we're going through is far more powerful than "You too can have all the answers!"

Ask the right questions.

Working with Muslim refugees in East Africa, I read J.D. Greear's *Breaking the Islam Code*. One of Greear's central premises is that Westerners often answer questions the Muslim mind and heart aren't asking. For example, Muslims don't ask if they can be forgiven. But they spend their entire lives seeking to be *clean*. Their hearts naturally long for more intimacy with God, since the nearest reference to closeness to Allah is a sura stating he is as close to them as a sword to their jugular vein.[6] (Whoa.)

In building relationships with people, we find out not what plug-and-play puzzle piece to apply, but instead understand, as with Nicodemus or Zacchaeus or the woman at the well, what they long for. Ask older kids about their friends who don't know Christ: What questions is this person's heart asking? What's under their anger, offense, or resistance? What are they really looking for?

Fresh Ink: Resources for Vibrant Faith

- Together, memorize verses that equip kids to talk about the gospel. Find 12 of them on free, printable memory cards from Seeds Family Worship's Seeds of Faith—then download the songs that go with them to make memorizing easy.

- Older kids might find Cru's "The Words" project intriguing, or their Soularium resource. They use words or pictures to help people tell their own story and jump-start spiritual conversations. To be clear, this could be a decent tool to help us *listen.*

- As good conversation starters with older kids, look up some videos on YouTube: "That Awkward Moment When You Try to Share Your Faith" from the Billy Graham Evangelism Association, and "Real Conversations" with Jonathan McKee.

True Colors: Discussion Questions for Kids

- Ask at least one person in your life, "How did you become a Christian? What factors did God use to bring you to him?"

- Why do we care about whether people know Jesus?

Think Ink: Contemplative Questions for Parents

- How often are you involved in actively sharing your faith through actions or words?
- What's your biggest obstacle in talking about Christ with others?
- Reflect on your own story of conversion. Ask yourself, *Do I believe that just like Jesus was able to bring me from death to life, he can exert the same power over the person I want to share him with?*

I suppose I understand the heart behind questions like "How many times did you share Jesus with someone this week?" But right now, that feels a little like someone asking about how often I talk about my husband or my kids.

I love them. They make me so happy I could spit. My life is full of them. To not talk about them would be weird—a curious declaration about my family or me or the listener. When it comes to my kids sharing their faith, in every way, I hope they love God enough to do so.

Prayer of the Dependent Parent

Lord, evangelism requires so much love: overflowing love for you and understanding of this gift of salvation, love for others that overwhelms our comfort and our agendas, that goes the distance to listen to people and the questions their hearts are asking.

Don't let us be a resounding gong or a clanging cymbal (1 Corinthians 13:1-3). Don't let us fear people instead of you (Galatians 1:10).

I pray for our family what Paul asked the Ephesians to pray for him: "That whenever I speak, words may be given me so that I will fearlessly make known the mystery of the gospel...Pray that I may declare it fearlessly, as I should" (6:19-20). Let us make the most of every opportunity (Ephesians 5:16), being trustworthy to express the mind-blowing hope of Christ in season and out of season (2 Timothy 4:2). Make us ready to gently and respectfully give an answer for the hope we have (1 Peter 3:15).

As we share, create patience and faith in us for your timing, your results. You feed many more than we expect from a few loaves and fishes. Any wins in sharing our faith are the work of your Spirit.

12

Resilience

Your Child, Stronger

My then 13-year-old and I sat across a sticky table from each other at the local donut shop. If I remember right, he held a maple-frosted thing that was the size of a small planet, totally at my permission (unusual for my sugar-nazi tendencies). His tears had dried by now, leaving a whisper of salt on ruddy cheeks.

"I just feel like I have more setbacks than wins." He shrugged heavily, as if wearing a backpack of rocks.

He wasn't entirely wrong. That was the day when out of the four saxophonists who auditioned for advanced band, three made it in. And it stunk to be number four.

Add to that the fact that he is my kid with a couple of learning disorders. He's come so far, people. But that means that out of my four kids, three of them find school relatively easy. One doesn't. (Sensing a pattern here?) And junior highers aren't particularly merciful when your ADHD lapses into *annoying* territory.

All that to say, my son was becoming good friends with striking out.

Permanent Truth

Resilience is about:

- pressing through pain—and into it—with gratitude and trust, rather than avoiding or denying it
- valuing and pursuing the sizable gifts and character acquired in darkness
- waiting patiently to see God's goodness and character we know is there
- preparing kids to fully grieve and yet get up again after life's inevitable losses—including those we can't see yet

Watching him across the table from me, I glimpsed a sense of powerlessness. He was working out an answer to that lifelong question, "Where is God in my pain?"

My heart wanted to scoop him up like when he was little, cuddle him, and let him laugh out loud at *Clifford the Big Red Dog* on TV. (But maybe that would contribute to a teenager's sense of failure. Ya know.)

How can we help our kids deal? By teaching resilience. And allowing what precedes it.

Wrestlers, Cancer, and How Your Child's Pain Could Be a Gift

A friend of mine, Marshall, is six foot three. He was upward of 190 pounds as a high school wrestler back in the day. Maybe that's why I was surprised at who he said were the most formidable in the sport: the kids from the school for the blind. In fact, one of them was the state champ during Marshall's years in competition. At the time, wrestling and swimming were the only sports available to those students; baseball, basketball, and football were all out. So they practiced and competed year-round.

What mattered even more, though, was that wrestlers who are blind have a heightened sense of touch. We've all heard that with the loss of one of our senses, our other senses rally to compensate (think of Stevie Wonder or Ray Charles). *Scientific American* reports that the brain rewires itself to boost the other senses. It's a phenomenon now known as cross-modal neuroplasticity: "If one sense is lost, the areas of the brain normally devoted to handling that sensory information do not go unused—they get rewired and put to work processing other senses."[1]

This got me thinking. Could the loss of something we desperately want gain something we don't yet know we desperately need?

Rewired in Struggle

This conversation about wrestling caught me bewildered at a soul level from a cancer scare with our son Will, which happened around his thirteenth birthday. But I was also reflecting on his remarkable response of faith like a lion, which occasionally outpaced my own belief. Even as we wept together, that boy started talking about what he was thankful for. He said things like, "God has a good plan for this. And even if I die, I get to be with Jesus, right?" Or when I couldn't stop crying the next morning: "I have complete faith that God has a good plan for this. God had a plan for Henry (our recently passed toddler friend). And God has a plan for me. I mean, he's not the kind of God who goes around giving people tumors for fun."

Someone had once told me that Abraham, when asked to sacrifice his son, hadn't received the faith he needed like some supernatural shot in the arm. Faith was something built. Though a lot of people liken faith to a muscle, John pointed out that maybe it's more like rappelling. Perhaps faith is more about loosening our death grip on the rope and realizing the breathtaking freedom of leaning back into trust.

The day Will, John, and I traveled for the MRI and oncologist consultation, I felt like Abraham going up the mountain. *Lord, he is yours. But why this?* I kept waiting for a rustle in the bushes, some sort of ram I wasn't promised to receive.

Will slumped as we waited for the necessary two hours, whining about drinking the chalky oral contrast. Into my red journal, I copied words from Shadrach, Meshach, and Abednego, their words of trust-filled release: "If we are thrown into the blazing furnace, the God we serve is able to deliver us from it, and he will deliver us from Your Majesty's hand. *But even if he does not,* we want you to know, Your Majesty, that we will not serve your gods or worship the image of gold you have set up" (Daniel 3:17-18, emphasis added).

Following the longest six weeks of my life, doctors concluded our son actually had an extra cervical rib—not, as they thought, lymphoma. Something thought to be a lymph node was a muscle; another swelling was a normal thymus gland. (Did you even know you had a thymus gland?) Will decided to affectionately name his newly discovered rib "Eve."

But John and I had already wondered in conversation, *Where did this kid develop such a capability to place this in God's arms?*

As we talked, the most obvious was Will's diagnosis of ADHD at age five, followed later by dysgraphia. (Irony: The son of a writer labors painfully to write or spell *anything*. He has been counseled to strictly *type* any future love letters.) No book has a word count high enough to communicate the tears (his and mine) over his former mortifying lack of self-control, and his playdates where I doled out strategized rewards for not melting down or hitting anyone. He and I muscled through spelling lists two years behind his grade level. Countless prayers were offered, pleadings made, and systems established.

Mind you, we are still a work in progress. But Will is now my most resilient child. I have discovered such gratitude for the ways these disorders have grown our family.

Imagine the tears I swallowed when his eyes lit up with the topic choice for his first school speech: "The Treasures of ADHD." His conclusion? *I am glad for the way I am. I am still amazed by the way God made me.*

Less than six months after that diagnosis, our family moved to Africa. We were maddeningly, frequently without power or Internet or water—built-in delays of gratification (for all of us, doggone it). If my kids purchased a Lego set, it would arrive in three or four months with an intern.

I tell you this not to glorify suffering. But you've likely read of "snowplow parents" aiming to bulldoze every obstacle from a child's path. Experts speculate that this approach results in kids ill-prepared for adulthood.

The Stories We Tell Ourselves

I had to learn early on to watch my language, so to speak, when it came to tough stuff—because the narratives we tell ourselves and our kids do matter, especially in the tough times. And in Tim Keller's words, if we get the story wrong, we get our response wrong.[2]

So until my son was old enough to more fully appreciate his strengths and uniqueness—and not to use his disorders as a crutch—we referred (with attempted hope and a neutral-to-positive tone of voice) to "the way God made your brain."

Your kids pick up on a lot of what you think about something by the ways you talk about it. Your goal shouldn't be to move your child into denial or overlook their anguish, but rather to communicate hope and trust in the way God is writing their story.

We attach different values based on story. Take some collectors' computers from 1977 that were assembled in a garage and signed inside by Steve Wozniak and Steve Jobs. Obsolete—even useless—as the actual computers may be, one sold for $650,000.[3]

Story often equals value.

How we respond to our kids' experience of hardship helps shape that story. Sometimes this means acknowledging our kids' core emotion, giving them permission to grieve. One night in Uganda, my kids watched their grandparents swallowed into yet another airport. Our kids were weeping. John leaned over. "Some people told me when I was a kid not to be sad. But I want you to cry. It says something about how valuable your grandparents are to you, and that's a good thing."

Songwriter Michael Card remarks, "Jesus understood that lament was the only true response of faith to the brokenness and fallenness of the world."[4] Sometimes kids need to hear, "It is right and just that you should be upset about something that's wrong."

Sure, some kids will tend toward waterworks rather than resilience. But when the grief or anger or outright fear is real, take a beat to recognize what isn't right about this world.

Outside Lazarus's tomb, Jesus was well aware of what God purposed to do in the next few minutes. But first he rage-cried (as per the meaning of the Greek word, elsewhere used to express indignance, rage, and stern warning). He didn't say that because God was going to do something good, and therefore Lazarus's death was good.[5]

At times, I have not fully grieved what is wrong about this world—not mourned with God—because somehow I've become convinced a joyful Christian is not sad or discouraged or ticked. In all honesty, I think this has stilted my relationship with God, my wholehearted worship of him, because I could bring only the parts of me that had their act together (we're getting down to the single percentages that qualify, people). I have been a plasticky sort of Christian—one that even my kids could see right through.

Christian joy isn't some version of looking like Barbie, with the eternal smile that can't be wiped off: *Well, God said to rejoice! Have a cookie.* It acknowledges that "we are afflicted in every way, but not crushed; perplexed, but not driven to despair; persecuted, but not forsaken; struck down, but not destroyed" (2 Corinthians 4:8-10 ESV). It says, *I have deep, abiding happiness in God that surrounds me in hope and peace and belief, even when I can't see through my own tears.* These seeds of God's presence with us in pain sprout the monumental gift of compassion in our kids, of comforting others with the comfort we've received (2 Corinthians 1:4).

Instead of choosing to believe God's goodness and make an offering of worship in the midst of uncomfortable, even piercing emotion, I have been guilty of pretending that pain isn't there. That's when I haven't modeled for my kids what honoring God looks like in the full spectrum of emotion. We want instead to invite kids to bring their most intense questions about God right to him and right into our worship. (Suffering, after all, is a big part of God's own identity—because he loves much. I don't want to keep my kids from that aspect of understanding him, either.)

Will our kids tell their stories as recipients of a bad rap, considering what they "deserve"? Overlooked, suck-it-up-buttercup pawns of a cosmic Being's plans that care nothing for them? Or will they tell their stories as beloved children of God, laden with purpose, his heart breaking first in their pain?

Hunting for Plan B

Kids need our help to gain perspective on failure or loss. That said, failing an advanced band audition does not mean one's primary life path is closed.

In our conversation at the donut shop, I asked my son if he remembered the waterslide we screamed down the previous summer.

Where had the engineer designed all the water to go? (The pool at the bottom.) Did it all end up there? (Mom, c'mon.) We talked about the verse from Proverbs: "In the LORD's hand the king's heart is a stream of water that he channels toward all who please him" (21:1). If there had been a hole in the waterslide, the water would have drained out to the wrong place. God shuts doors—boarding up the slide, so to speak—so the water of our life goes to all the right places.

My son and I dreamed a little bit. What could my son be good at instead? What other possibilities might be open because this door closed? My son needed a little help from a more developed frontal lobe (that is, mine), so we talked about what was going right, things in which he hadn't failed. We talked about life-altering things that, by the grace of God, my son has going for him. He has thriving health, a family who's crazy about him, a warm home, a love for cooking mouthwatering food, and killer compassion.

Honesty is critical here but can get tricky. Obviously, we don't want to go with a shrug and say, "Well, if you would have practiced more..." But part of the gift of failure (yes, I called it that) is our human ability to change. After the dreaming together and accumulated positive rapport, I asked, "Is there something you wish you would have done differently?" Or you could say, "Is there something you wish you could go back and change?"

It's that classic adage of parents around the world: You can't change their action; you can only change your reaction.

Kids who expect that the world should rightfully hand them perfection are in for a rude awakening. We want to raise resilient kids—problem-solvers who seize responsibility for their own capacity to change.

So help them dream about plan B. I asked my son questions about what he hoped to do in life with his instrument. What was his end game? What did he like about band? Should he try another elective better suited to what he's good at? Should he try out for jazz band instead? What practical steps would it take to get to plan B? He decided to talk with his teacher about what went wrong and about what he'd need to do if he wanted to do band in high school.

Maybe Don't Do This: A Beginning List

Don't just distract them. Yes, sometimes they'll need help to snap out of it. (A donut? Did I suggest that?) But communicate that being angry, sad, or afraid is okay, and that you'll sit with them through those feelings.

That said, *don't let them wallow.* In a way still respectful of their grief, provide your kids with healthy strategies for taking captive their thoughts (2 Corinthians 10:5). You're establishing patterns for how to deal with painful days in the future: the unfair boss, the project that blows up in their face, the kids who won't listen.

Don't focus on what everyone else did wrong. "I wish that teacher had seen your talent" makes the problem about someone else and surrenders our kids' capacity to change, grow, and learn. Imagine being that parent who, when the school calls about what's not going right, refrains from excuses or blaming in favor of working together toward more character in your child.

Don't always shield them from disappointments ("Oh, shoot! Her grandparents can't take her to the movies! I'd better think of a great stand-in!") *or others' suffering.* Take them to the funeral, the shelter, the sick person's bedside. Age-appropriately, talk about situations where you have no answers for your kids' whys—and your pervasive trust in God amid situations he chooses not to "fix."

Don't be afraid to *fix your mind on the future* (Colossians 3:2-3). Create heaven-lovers. Read books about heaven. Talk about it. Imagine a little. In the car or eating dinner, we used to play "I wonder if heaven has..."—which with little kids meant everything from puppies to rainbow slides to swimming pools of whipped cream. Either way, heaven will be better than whatever they dream up (see 1 Corinthians 2:9). This meant when a relative passed away, one of my kids talked like that person was one lucky dog. Another child simply talked about him in heaven as if the relative were visiting Disneyland.

This is not to spare kids internalizing the pain of losing someone. But our suffering on planet Earth is mitigated by the greatness of our reward. It's a reward God doesn't blush about or cover up. Let's talk up that reward to our kids, helping them visualize it while they're most able.

Don't accomplish plan B for them. Restore their sense of "I can" by showing them they have the ability to dig themselves out of whatever hole they fall into. I agreed to e-mail my son's band teacher (without a guilt trip) so we could devise strategies, but my son had a list of action points all his own.

Plan B

Whether on the mountaintops or in the valleys, we want our kids to have hope. Dr. Brené Brown calls hope "a function of struggle."[6] This echoes Scripture: "We know that suffering produces perseverance; perseverance, character; and character, hope" (Romans 5:3-4). Our plan B may just be God's plan A. In truth, he is all over our plan B. He's why we hope at all. Hope in God, the psalms compel us over and over.

God makes plan B airtight because even if plan B doesn't materialize, he channels me right where I'm created to be. He's going to be there, rooting for me and his glory even if it all unspools to plan Q (see Romans 8:31). Plan B (or Q) happens not because I ducked and let God kick me there. He uses the way I'm made, the things I long for, the passions that fuel me.

Grieving and disappointment set up our kids for a lifetime of walking with God as we follow Jesus into death—the death of ourselves. Father Thomas Keating remarks, "The spiritual journey is not a career or a success story. It is a series of humiliations of the false self that become more and more profound."[7] We see the example of Jesus, who turned toward his cross and its eventual joy (Hebrews 12:2) rather than sprinting from it. In Luke 9:51, as he moved into the week before his death, he "resolutely set out for Jerusalem."

Understandably, you'll choose at times whether to remove your child from a challenging, destructive situation or allow them the critical teaching experience—and emotional muscle—of learning from hard stuff as they work each situation out.

What gifts could God long to fold into your child's palms?

What if our children *not* having something, or encountering barriers or pain, causes faith and gratitude and perseverance to cycle into high gear? Will's habit of trusting God, I understand now, was just ratcheted up a level.

By all means, my son is not getting it all right. But this is what I want more than a straight-A student, or even one who makes the first cut in advanced band: a child with a heightened sense of God.

I watched my friend progress through the nightmare of her husband's stage-four kidney cancer this year. From diagnosis to the day she became a widow—and single mother of three—took just over 100 days. One night, as I transferred the children to their grandparents and we lamented the agony of their reality, her mother remarked she could still see my friend running around in footie pajamas as a child. I realized we never know what resilience our kids might need in the future for which today must prepare them.

Writing on the Wall: Practical Ideas

Encourage your kids to develop a "courage playlist."

Explain that this will be for days that require a little extra strength. As long as our songs have solid theology, this isn't just bravado and puffing up emotion; music is a great way to catechize ourselves as we rehearse truth.

Pop popcorn.

Have kids smell and maybe taste uncooked kernels. How does popcorn start tasting and smelling so good? Ask, "What in life can be compared to the heat needed to make the popcorn burst open?" Pop the corn, and as you enjoy it, talk about how heat helps us "blossom"—and even nurture those around us.[8]

Use modeling clay to teach flexibility.

Roll three small balls and one larger ball of modeling clay (not Play-Doh).[9] Give the smaller balls three names to represent people, and explain the struggles in their lives. ("People make fun of Emilio at school.") I think it could be visually useful to squash the balls a little bit! Shape the bigger ball into a simple canoe, put it in water, and watch it float—explaining that by staying flexible and open to stretching, we can help other people. (Drop the other poor little squashed clay balls in the canoe.)

Write hidden messages.

Using a cotton swab and milk or lemon juice, write "God is my strength" on a piece of white paper. (If you have multiple kids, you could give each a paper with a hidden message: "God's plans are always good." "God cares for me." "God is my safe place.") Allow it to dry. Talk to your kids about how tough times expose what's in us—and hopefully, the "hidden truths" God has written on our hearts. Do they see anything that makes this piece of paper different from another? (No.) When they hold the paper over a lightbulb—the heat, literally and metaphorically—can they read the hidden message?

Reward courageous steps.

A small step for a child without challenges may be a giant leap for a struggling child ("You went to church today without throwing a fit!" "You had an entire day without an outburst!"). Together, adjust your expectations for a challenged child's new "normal." Cheer them on! Look up and write down all the staggering promises in Revelation 2–3 for overcomers. And get ready to be conquerors together.

Ask kids to create their own board game.

This could be similar to Life or Chutes and Ladders and include obstacles they face socially, physically, and intellectually. Perhaps players have to surmount these obstacles by fulfilling a small challenge.

Watch for clues about emotional difficulties.

Kids' behavior can signal their need for support with emotional difficulties. Watch for clues about those difficulties, asking yourself...

- What brings tears to their eyes? I watch for even the exact triggering phrase. Help your kids learn to acknowledge what they feel and to know their own signals: "I see that you're getting easily frustrated. Sometimes I get cranky when I'm tired. Think you might be feeling tired?"

- What reactions seem disproportionate? These can be indicators of the iceberg hovering beneath the surface. If I see someone acting in a more powerful way than the situation demands, I could get distracted by the way they're expressing themselves and miss the *why* throbbing beneath.

- What statements do they repeat? How do you know when they're tired? When you were a new parent, you learned to distinguish their tired, angry, and hungry cries. Do the same for them now.

- What do they not want to talk about? Pray about when to press in and when to give space, particularly when they could use time to cool off.

- What is precious to my child that's being lost or trampled on? Ask gently probing questions to help your child uncover the answer. Asking questions helps us isolate the pain point (and sometimes, in anger, the heart idol that has become too precious, morphing from desire to demand).

- What stories do they tell? This can be tough with kids who tell a lot of mundane stories crowded with belabored details. But stories are hand-selected pieces of their day that feel meaningful. Why did they choose to tell these stories? Are the common threads people they admire or moments they find memorable? What are you learning about your kids' values, social skills, and their curated world?

- What could their bodies be telling you? Sometimes a tummy ache is just a tummy ache, insomnia means lying awake like any other kid in town might be, and a fit is a call for discipline. But when does a tummy ache signal anxiety or a fake sickness? How late has a child been on screens? Could that angry outburst be a hangry or exhausted, at-my-limits outburst?

Fresh Ink: Resources for Vibrant Faith

- I like Beverly Lewis's beautifully illustrated *What Is Heaven Like?* as well as Randy Alcorn's *Heaven for Kids* and *Tell Me About Heaven*.

- Another to try out: Lysa TerKeurst's *It Will Be Okay: Trusting God Through Fear and Change*.

True Colors: Discussion Questions for Kids

- How do you think God feels when we're hurt or sad?

- What are some of the reasons he still allows difficult things to happen? (Check out John 9:1-3; 11:1-7,32-45; James 1:2-4; and Romans 5:3-5. Job 1 is a fascinating chapter to go through with older kids.)

Think Ink: Contemplative Questions for Parents

- In the story of Jesus raising Lazarus, in John 11:38, the Greek term *embrimáomai* is often translated "deeply moved" (NIV, HCSB, ESV). Yet the use of the term elsewhere in Scripture and in the immediate context suggests a different meaning: typically, an expression of rage, rebuke, indignation, and anger.[10] Take a minute to revisit a time when you did not feel like God showed up: a situation where the outcome felt dead, maybe with a huge rock thrown in front.

- How does this picture of Jesus, angry at what is wrong in this world (despite knowing he would conquer what's wrong, creating beauty from it), affect your interpretation of what happened? What if Christ was angry and weeping *with* you?

- How does your past pain affect how you guide your kids to deal with failure, loss, and hurt?

Prayer of the Dependent Parent

Lord, as much as this walk with you is full of goodness, we follow you into death of ourselves (Galatians 2:20). On this planet, we can anticipate loss, pain, suffering, persecution, and failure. Shape us in readiness for adversity—to weather it with strength and trust and wholehearted honesty, turning toward you rather than away.

We sense this even in parenting: suffocating disappointment, fear, some of our most terrifying nightmares materializing into reality. The pain of parenting, as you well know, is real.

Thank you that our suffering is not purposeless. Thank you that your way is to give more than you take, that your way is always and ultimately resurrection and restoration of far more than you ask of us. Cause us to love you for more than your gifts. Create in us and train us in your unfailing hope.

13

Respecting Authority

Stepping Down

I've been putting off writing this chapter.

It's because creating a sense of respect in my kids still feels like having my fingernails plucked off one by one. With teenagers, our family is reteaching respect. And in response to my exasperation, John recently laughed; he thinks "obedient children" can occasionally be an oxymoron. Teaching obedience requires so much doggone *vigilance*, including consistency, rapport, and involvement.

American culture demands very little of my kids in this area. Our country was actually founded on some degree of rebellion. Yet previous generations and other global cultures have tended to expect more respect from kids. Some of those would be mildly horrified by the manners of some American children toward their parents. So I try to dial it back a few decades in my expectations of my kids.

But then again, previous generations tended to use shame as a motivator in a way we recognize as destructive today. Still, we can solidly establish respect without shaming children, though it's harder to do without wielding a sense of disconnection and unworthiness based on our kids' behavior.

Respect is what we see as God draws us near in the New Testament, apart from our obeying his law. Paul says that when we try to prove our worthiness by obedience, we "have been *alienated* from Christ" (Galatians 5:4, emphasis added). But, he continues, instead of viewing our nearness to God as a license to disobey, "do not use your freedom to indulge the flesh; rather, serve one another humbly in love" (verse 13).

Our kids are going to be under authority their entire lives. Except for a few horrid dictators of suffering countries, everyone on this planet is under earthly authority of some kind. (Even Jesus was under authority: "Very truly I tell you, the Son can do nothing by himself; he can do only what he sees his Father doing," says Jesus of himself in John 5:19.) And while most of us live in countries with voted-in officials, Scripture asserts, "Let everyone be subject to the governing authorities, for there is no authority except that which God has established. The authorities that exist have been established by God. Consequently, whoever rebels against the authority is rebelling against what God has instituted, and those who do so will bring judgment on themselves...For the one in authority is God's servant for your good" (Romans 13:1-2,4).

When we require kids to respect authority, it's in part because we don't want our kids to be in rebellion to God's authority or his agents. The only time they shouldn't be obeying is when an authority figure's command falls contrary to God's. Think of Rahab protecting the spies (Joshua 2), Daniel and his friends worshipping only God (Daniel 3 and 6), the Magi reneging on their promise to return to Herod (Matthew 2), or Peter and John rejecting the Pharisees' authority in order to tell people about Jesus (Acts 4:1-22).

That said, our days are stuffed with opportunities for kids to practice respectful submission: when they're pulled over for a traffic stop, when they report to a teacher who could pave the way for their personal thriving or land them in the principal's office, when they're holding down a job, or when they need to honor someone who isn't personally honorable. Offering our kids the gift of submission to and respect for authority is one of those keys that opens doors for the rest of their lives.

Obedience: Following the Leader

In practice for worship band, next to all my parts on the sheet music, I once scrawled *4"*. This was my shorthand to hold the mic four inches from my mouth whenever I sang harmony—to keep harmony second tier. Otherwise, I obliterate other musicians.

Any sound engineer will tell you that sound that grabs your heart from your chest involves just the right volume of each element. I hold the mic farther away when I sing harmony because it is often disordered and discordant when it sits at the same volume as melody.

Just as in a dance, one leads, the other follows. One is not more important than the other. They're still in lockstep, working together. But following the lead matters. We're training kids in the freedom of God's proper order.

Worse than a Rebel

Kids learn how to obey God from how they obey us. So expecting respect from my kids is based on my God-given role to teach them how to obey God. What if I don't teach this? Well, imagine the behavior that's tacky in a three-year-old on full display in a fifteen-year-old, when it's much harder to control and the possibility of life-altering havoc looms large and real.

Yet, even in that obedience, we don't seek sin management but holistic heart change and knowledge of God's ways. God speaks of the Israelites, whom he brought out of Egypt: "Your ancestors tested and tried me, though for forty years they saw what I did. That is why I was angry with that generation; I said, 'Their hearts are always going astray, and *they have not known my ways*'" (Hebrews 3:9-10, emphasis added).

If our kids know and see God's works but don't know *him*, it's a little like knowing your spouse on paper: their favorite coffee drink, their clothing size, the way they like their eggs. But if you didn't know why their shoulders slump when they walk in from work or why your teenager makes them feel fear or what makes their heart leap, you'd be missing *your spouse*.

Permanent Truth

We willingly place ourselves below those God puts in charge because we trust the order he puts things in. Respecting authority is about:

- not grumbling
- not excusing poor leadership
- showing respect for a person in all their imperfection
- comprehending the weight leaders carry
- learning to obey and trust God like Sarah and Abigail and early Christians did, even when we can't see him sticking up for us
- knowing how to form a "respectful plea"
- responding from the heart, even in the absence of corresponding emotion

Most kids are primed to impress their parents. (I was good at this.) Read: You may not have a rebel. But a Pharisee could be worse. Yes, normal and healthy kids long for our kudos. Motivation by praise is a God-inlaid part of us (think "Well done, good and faithful servant"). But God also has much to say to people (like me) who crave the accolades of people disproportionately. He says that the Pharisees "loved human praise more than praise from God" (John 12:43). Author Tedd Tripp cautions, "A change in behavior that does not stem from a change in heart is not commendable; it is *condemnable*. Is it not the hypocrisy that Jesus condemned in the Pharisees?...Yet this is what we often do in childrearing. We demand changed behavior and never address the heart that drives the behavior."[1]

We can follow the lead of God, who doesn't just discipline us every time we do wrong. He parents our hearts.

Inside-Out Respect

What could it look like to focus on raising kids willing to follow from the inside out? Here are some general ways we can train our kids in respect.

Discipline differently for childish behavior as opposed to outright rebellion.

One time I found out one of my preteens had been spitting cherry pits *onto the kitchen floor*. After my brief cardiac arrest, I had to admit this was kids being (self-centered, lazy, irresponsible, airheaded) kids. It wasn't malicious or defiant.

Differentiate between the request and the tone.

We want kids to know it's okay to come to us for sibling arbitration or more apple juice. But if it's presented in a tacky way, we can respond evenly, as if from a script: "You're not allowed to speak to me that way." I say this at least twice a day (sigh).

Peer beneath the surface of compliant older kids.

Having *control* over our kids isn't the same as developing their ability to decisively shoulder responsibility for their own moral choices. The authors of *The Cure & Parents* assert, "In an environment where parents only impose rules through their child's adolescence, it can thwart and stunt them from learning to own their choices. So a compliant, immature child grows into a compliant, immature young adult. When they discover imposed life choices didn't work, they have no one to hold responsible but their parents."[2]

As a compliant teenager, I found college overwhelming because I no longer had anyone to tell me what to do and how to do it. So I became a generalized people-pleaser instead.

Rebellious kids can be overwhelming and downright frightening. But kids who just do what they're told may not internalize their own relationship with Christ or assert their own moral character outside of what others tell them to do.

Crack down on the interruptions.

This reinforces listening rather than our kids' own agendas. We don't interrupt authority figures (or people in general), and that includes parents.

Don't let your kids divide your unified front.

If you have an issue with your spouse's parenting, when possible, confront this in private, and if necessary, your spouse can return to your child and repent.

Kids also need to know that if they go to one parent for permission to do something, you're both on the same page. They're not allowed to go to the other parent for a different answer. Show them that you respect each other, and they need to respect your relationship as well. All of this can be especially important—and tricky—with blended families in their heightened quest for unity.

If we see an increase in bad attitudes, we sometimes take away media.

Media may not always be the cause; my kids can do bad all by themselves. But I want my kids to see the connection between their input and their output. Banning certain media tends to be a consequence that's particularly painful (in a good way) for my kids.

Align expectations with your child's development.

If you asked your four-year-old to accomplish five things and they didn't, that may be more than their working memory can hold at one time. And a teenager won't have a fully developed frontal lobe (responsible for judgment and memory, among other things) until around age *25*, so set expectations accordingly. Think about what's reasonable to ask of your kids (and have you taught them how to do it?). Communicate that home is an okay place to learn and make mistakes.

We don't want AI children who mindlessly obey.

Sometimes I need my kids' input too. I teach them the "respectful plea"—a "script" to respectfully disagree. It might sound like, *Mom, I understand that you _____. Can I offer a different perspective? Because of _____, I think _____.* But they have to be okay with a no even after I reconsider.

I frequently quote author Ginger Hubbard's mantra to my kids: "Obey all the way, right away, with a joyful heart."[3] This encompasses the standard to which I want to hold them and will influence how they respect other authority in their lives.

Respect your spouse.

Stick up for each other in front of the kids. Someone might ask, "What if my spouse isn't acting respectably?" For every person in authority, God still asks us to respect their position. Romans 13:1-7 was written when Nero was burning Christians as torches in his gardens.

Discipline with consequences rather than tone of voice.

Say you receive a letter from the IRS about an error in your taxes. The letter is in a completely neutral tone of voice; there are no exclamation points or irate language. But the potential consequences speak for themselves (and perhaps increase your blood pressure).

Motivate the rebels.

Author Gretchen Rubin offers advice that has been critical for my family in motivating the rebels among us (both tall ones and short ones): "For Rebels, the most effective habit-change strategy is the Strategy of Identity. Because Rebels place great value on being true to themselves, they can embrace a habit if they view it as a way to express their identity. 'I quit sugar because I respect my body. I want to give myself energy and good health by eating only healthy foods.'"[4]

God made rebels for a purpose. Who's to say your child doesn't need that force of will to teach in an inner-city school someday? Live among an unreached people group? Help end human trafficking? Withstand persecution? Your child's spirit doesn't need to be broken. Just help that spirit love God's leadership and authority.

Heart change and true submission to God and others are brought about only as our kids (and we ourselves) sincerely seek forgiveness from God and, because of his Holy Spirit, are given hearts of flesh rather than stone (Ezekiel 11:19). God is clear that he alone gives the Spirit of wisdom and revelation in the knowledge of him (Ephesians 1:17). So, renovating kids' hearts is ultimately something we only prepare the soil for, as we wait for God to give the growth. He's the one who softens hearts as he chooses (Romans 9:14-18).

Writing on the Wall: Practical Ideas

Role-play situations where kids will need to obey in the future.

For younger kids, you could use stuffies, dolls, or puppets (bonus points if you make them together with paper sacks or socks). Imagine some hurdles to obey. The puppet says, "Hmm. I don't want to obey. I want to _____. What should I do? What does God want me to do?"

If the condition persists over time, the consequences worsen.

Key parenting technique from my father-in-law: If the behavior doesn't eventually respond to discipline, provided there aren't underlying issues, the "fire" of the consequences turns up to lay on a little more heat.

Know your kids' pain points.

Hint: This usually means taking away something they love. Baden loathes separation from his phone. Will and Jack immediately backpedal on disobedience when I take away screens (whereas Corinne couldn't care less). Corinne loves alone time, so when she receives an extra chore, she gives me a gaze that could jackhammer concrete. (You might think different consequences for different kids threatens justice, but it's not equal pain if a child's consequence costs them nothing.)

Consider presenting moral decisions to them as choices, with a list of consequences.

As Joshua offered the Israelites: "Choose for yourselves this day whom you will serve" (Joshua 24:15). Locking yourself in a battle of wills turns your child more against you, making it personal, rather than helping them acknowledge their own choices and contributions. Disobedience is a choice, but not a good one—and we don't want to shield kids from its consequences.

Repetition matters.

Someone once asked me to estimate how many times I told my toddlers they needed to say "please" or "thank you." When I thought about it, I realized I was saying it at least 27 times a day. And at 365 days a year—because there ain't no days off—they still didn't have it ingrained until they were probably four or five. So after 9,855 times a year for five years, I get 49,275 times. (You're thinking, *Is she meaning this to be encouraging?*) It takes so much time and repetition to change even the smallest tendencies of the human heart. Teaching respect takes time too.

Get out your kids' train track set.

Tell them that obedience is like a railroad track. A train may think it has freedom by being able to go wherever it wants, but it's only safe when it's on the tracks.

Use a basic sticker chart.

Even smiley faces or frowny faces on a whiteboard can help a child visualize and be rewarded for obedience. Be careful this doesn't stray into humiliation or shaming if kids start comparing themselves with one another. Little kids need more immediate rewards, so you might reward your three-year-old for five stickers instead of fifteen.

For more activity ideas, discussion questions, and other resources for teaching kids how to respect authority, visit janelbreitenstein.com/permanentmarkers/respectingauthority.

Fresh Ink: Resources for Vibrant Faith

For older kids:

- Try biographies like Corrie ten Boom's *The Hiding Place* and Barbara Rainey's *Growing Together in Courage*. These provoke discussions about authority, ethics, and when it might be wrong to obey.

- Read Martin Luther King Jr.'s "Letter from a Birmingham Jail" (available online). In his letter, King asks, "How does one determine whether a law is just or unjust?" and lays out his biblical justification for nonviolent protest. Follow this by watching *John Lewis: Good Trouble*.

Try these picture books with younger kids:

- *Do Unto Otters* by Laurie Keller
- Any of the Jane Yolen and Mark Teague *How Do Dinosaurs...?* books

True Colors: Discussion Questions for Kids

- What are the main reasons you think people don't want to obey? What attitudes are at the core of disobedience and disrespect?

- Are there any good reasons not to obey? Can you think of times in history when people definitely should have disobeyed?

- Read the story of Abigail in 1 Samuel 25. How did she deal with being under a foolish authority figure? What do you admire? Who else was sticking up for Abigail?

- Compare the attitudes of Satan in Isaiah 14:12-15 and Jesus in

Philippians 2:5-8. Then look at the outcomes of each. What's the difference?

- When should you obey other kids?

Think Ink: Contemplative Questions for Parents

- In what situations do you find it hardest to submit to an authority figure—or choose not to? In what ways do you need to examine your attitude against Scripture?

- What areas in obeying authority do you let slide? Speeding? Taxes? Using someone else's nontransferable season pass? Hiding a behavior your spouse has asked you not to do (see Ephesians 5:21)? Undermining church authority figures?

- Are there any ways you submit externally but not internally?

Parenting is full of many nightmarish days—days when discouragement swings you low. So, as we train kids in obedience, let's do it full of openhanded trust in the God who raises what appears to be dead.

Prayer of the Dependent Parent

Master, you took on the form of a servant. You obeyed to the point even of dying on a cross, and God exalted you for it (Philippians 2:5-8). You washed the feet of your disciples. And my kids and I need that kind of all-the-way obedience that's so contrary to this human condition of rebellion, selfishness, and superiority.

But it's supernatural. You alone rescue us from our arrogance and self-reliance. My own authority in my house often comes from my desire for control, my own kingdom, my own reactions, and fear of failure. Even as I seek to teach obedience, I rebel against you as King of my house.

Grant me the courage and vigilance to teach and require respect of my kids that's consistent with kingdom culture rather than my own. Help my kids think wisely about when they shouldn't obey an evil authority. And expose whether my kids' obedience proceeds from their hearts or some other motive.

I ask you to soften my kids' hearts, bowing them down to you from the inside. Let them willingly choose you as Lord and truly enjoy submissively knowing and loving you.

Confession and Repentance

Regrets Only

This story ranks in our family lore. My sister-in-law had spied her daughter picking at a hole in the kitchen screen door to the point that the hole grew—an act she'd specifically asked her kids not to do.

She huddled the children together in hopes of a confession. "Today's a special day, guys—a free day." For several minutes, she spoke of the substantial weight of not confessing what we do wrong and how liberating it feels to tell someone. "So today, you can tell me anything you've done wrong. I won't get mad, and you won't get in trouble."

"We won't get in trouble?" her son asked.

"Nope," she said, smiling graciously.

Her son's grin grew. He confessed all sorts of goodies that raised her eyebrows. The way she tells it, they must have tumbled out as if from an overturned gumball machine.

"You can't get angry," he reminded her, and continued with his litany.

"Have anything you'd like to confess?" my sister-in-law asked her daughter.

Her daughter shrugged mildly. "Nope."

Permanent Truth

We set a climate in our relationships for regularly, humbly allowing God to expose what's in our hearts. Confession is about:

- agreeing with God about our sin—that, like cancer, it must be found and cut out
- increasing our affection for God as we realize how much we're forgiven and loved
- admitting we messed up, needing first vertical (Godward) forgiveness, reconciliation, and restoration, then horizontal (with others), in a circle of individuals reaching as far as the offense
- taking responsibility for both the heart attitude and the specific wrong action(s) that came from it
- intentionally changing future behavior
- accepting our consequences[1]

Her son continued his confessional. "Remember! You can't get angry!" His sister remained passive, even bored. *Got nothin'.*

That's the funny thing about confession. As with every other life skill—but perhaps most obviously here—we can't force a sincere response. We can cultivate an atmosphere where those responses could appear, but like the difference between my attempts to garden in Illinois and in the deer-infested, mountain desert of Colorado, every soil is different. And as Paul asserts, "I planted the seed, Apollos watered it, but God has been making it grow" (1 Corinthians 3:6). Only One creates that new life inside.

This is the mantra God whispers in my ear as I wrangle the problem child of the hour and as I write this book: *Even solid parenting can only go so far.*

But what does our due diligence in "planting" look like? How can we steer our kids' hearts toward confession and repentance?

When the One Who Needs to Apologize Is Me

I struggle with parent rage. (Coincidentally, it's an issue about one week out of the month. It's my trusty, though inexcusable, sin pattern.)

Take the week we'd had with family for John's milestone birthday—which was fabulous. It also meant that because of my party prep, by the time late Thursday night rolled around, I had not taken a break since 6:15 Monday morning. My helper-ad-nauseam personality type tends to totally ignore personal needs until they are unignorable, accelerating me from zero to 120 mph in 3.7 seconds.

Mom's meltdown started with a child perpetually running his hands over a squeaky balloon while I drove (audio stuff can drive me bonkers). Another child was on her third night of prebedtime tears. And, of course, another decided to pick at his current rival sibling.

Let's just say that if we had gotten a still shot of us around 9:27 p.m., my index finger would have been jabbing, my jaw steely, and my mouth stretched by drill-sergeant wrath. When the rage had mellowed and kids were burrowed into bed, I required a relational FEMA truck: first repenting of my behavior to God, then restoring my relationship with my kids.

I slept terribly. When 6:15 dawned, I woke each child with an apology and a firm hug, asking for forgiveness for the Mompocalypse. Later, before I shoveled them out the door for school, I led us in duly needed prayer and repentance (with tears of my own).

When my kids blow it—like we all did that night—I consistently seek to remind us: *I completely love you, even when you totally mess up. And thankfully, that's how God loves us. We need Jesus.*

I wish I could take away my eruptive lack of self-control or the way I morphed instantly into military mode. I wish I could erase what I'd modeled for my kids: *This is how a parent acts when they're exhausted and have had it up to here.* But what remained in my power were two words: *I'm sorry.*

Being a perfect parent is not the goal. Being a Jesus-loving, Jesus-needing parent—that's the goal.

Creating a Confession Culture

Author Paul David Tripp cautions that when we blame our kids or the circumstances for our own junk, we "are essentially saying: 'My problem isn't a heart problem; my problem is a poverty of grace problem. If only God had given me _____, I wouldn't have had to do what I did.'"[2]

Parents who are willing to openly own up to their wrongs—from the negligible to the capital—are more likely to possess deep humility. The more we get real about our sin, the more the gospel is real in our homes and the more likely our kids will be to adopt the same attitudes and behaviors.

We can cultivate an "I'm sorry/I forgive you" culture in our homes. Gently encourage your kids to take responsibility for what they do wrong—to declare war on their sin rather than blame-shifting. Talk openly about both strengths and weaknesses in ways that see everyone as being in process.

As a parent, model an eagerness to seek forgiveness from God, then others (your spouse is a consistent source!) for even the smallest infractions and a willingness to learn from anyone. What have you got to lose? (As a colleague of mine pointed out, "I was changing a diaper and got poop in my eyebrow last week. You can't get much lower than that.") We're not trying to hide or fake anything or hold a position of superiority. So, if you pray together before bedtime, consider taking 30 seconds to a minute to silently confess your sins to God—and to each other, if needed.

Before church in the car, sometimes our family takes a minute to silently ask God for specific forgiveness and then (à la Matthew 5:24) ask forgiveness from each other before we go and worship. Rather than coming to God with our mental résumé of all the good things we've done this week, we can show our kids, *This is how we get ourselves ready to receive God. We repent.* It's not unlike John the Baptist preparing the way—leveling the paths for Jesus through repentance (see Matthew 3:2-3).

Got Something in Your Eye?

One of my favorite moments from a Christmas break a while back found Corinne and me in my little sunroom, paintbrushes in hand. She was trying out her new easel. I was leaning against the love seat, watercoloring. A happy surprise was how much she shared about what was going on at school.

A memory that will stick with me even longer? Her observation about how she was contributing to the problem, not just how other girls were mishandling things.

Maybe it sounds weird to like that behavior. But don't we want kids who voluntarily shuck sin's blindfold? We want kids who, from constant practice, see the log in their own eye, who can step back from any situation and see how their sin contributes and destroys—so they can make it right. To help your kids see the logs in their eyes, keep in mind the circumstances that make our hearts most likely to be soft.

- The conversation should be away from the potential added shame of other people's eyes.
- Allow a child to wait for a moment to respond so their brains aren't in fight, flight, or freeze mode.
- Address them with calm tones: "A gentle answer turns away wrath, but a harsh word stirs up anger" (Proverbs 15:1).

- Ask a child to put aside fears of their consequence and instead to focus on the bigger issue of their heart. Sometimes, if a child is truly responsive (as opposed to an excellent actor), a greater consequence isn't as necessary.

- Ask questions designed to bring about ownership of the issue, rather than throwing out accusations or pitting ourselves against our kids.

- Praise what seems to be true repentance, rather than the appearance of it (check out 2 Corinthians 7:10-11).

- Restore the sense of connection by holding your child after a tough discipline moment, voicing your enjoyment of your relationship and your hope in your child—bringing the child metaphorically back "home" to you.

When a child isn't "feelin'" the apology, give them time to calm down and step away from their anger or indignation. But then, if they still don't want to reconcile, understand that performing a discipline still has value even when we don't "feel" it. Remind your child to not let it go unresolved in their heart. Sometimes we've decided to withhold a privilege if a child hasn't made relational stuff right.

Our kids can make a lot of horrible or idiotic decisions. And they will. But kids who are teachable and repentant? *That* we can work with.

Writing on the Wall: Practical Ideas

Help your kids understand the power of body language in confession.

You could verbalize "I'm sorry" in, like, 23 ways—probably 19 of them insincere. If kids can't make a sincere apology, you might have them wait a few minutes to cool down, then try again. Tips:

- Apologize for both your general attitude toward the person and the specific wrong action.

- Look the other person in the eye.

- Uncross your arms, since crossed arms can communicate hostility or separation.

- Use a tone of voice that communicates that you understand the other person's hurt. If the apologizer is doing this poorly, it can help to have them imagine being hurt in a similar way: "What if your sister had dumped juice on your sketchbook? How would you want her to apologize?"

I like the five As of confession from The Young Peacemaker[3]:

- **A**dmit what you did wrong. (I ask my kids to be specific about what they did wrong, and also to acknowledge the heart attitude they had.)

- **A**pologize for how your choice affected the other person.

- **A**ccept the consequences.

- **A**sk for forgiveness.

- **A**lter your choice in the future.

(Note: I also take another *A* from the adult version: **A**void using *if, but,* or *maybe* in your apology.)

Memorize verses that talk about confession.

Start with Psalm 32:1-5; 51:10; 139:23-24; Matthew 5:23-24; 1 John 1:9. Celebrate by playing hide-and-seek—then talk about things that are definitely *not* good to hide.

Use situations in your home to illustrate the need for frequent confession.

The next time a kid finds something gross in your house—something fuzzy in the fridge, a baby with a dirty diaper, an unflushed toilet—casually ask whether it really needs to be dealt with. Is it that big of a deal? What would happen if we didn't? Explain how frequent confession with God keeps our souls healthy too.

When you disinfect a skinned knee, talk about the similarity to confession.

If we don't ask God to clean our hearts, that "infection" could grow—and hurt far worse. (Check out Psalm 32:2-8.)

Man up.

Check your kids' Internet history, dig into sudden abandonments of friendships, and take seriously others' intimations of your kids' misbehavior. Sometimes when I've looked through my child's computer history, my heart has knocked in my chest. What if I found terrible things? What if I found out what my child was really like? Our fears and failed expectations about who our kids are (or our own failure) can keep us from being relentless about the sin that hurts them, which festers like gangrene until much more loss is required.

Encourage use of the one percent rule.

Start your kids' peace talks by encouraging them first to admit the "log in [their] own eye" (Matthew 7:4-5 ESV)—their personal contribution to the issue—and then to ask forgiveness. This approach cuts through a lot of the bickering. You may have heard some version of the one percent rule: Even if your contribution is only one percent of the problem, take one hundred percent responsibility for that one percent.

Get out a bunch of empty suitcases.

Read Hebrews 12:1 together. Ask kids to pick up as many suitcases as they can. While your kids hold the suitcases, ball up some scrap paper. "Let's say that for every piece of paper you can catch with your hands, you get a small reward"—one less chore, extra screen time. How hard is it for your kids to receive the good things you're trying to give them? Explain that it's hard for us to "catch" the good gifts God has for us when we haven't turned over the baggage of our sin. He might have better relationships for us, for example, but we're not willing to let go of our destructive patterns. He might know that our lives will be good when we obey, but we're not willing to repent from laziness or disrespect.[4]

Try a clever object lesson from KidsOfIntegrity.com.

Ask your kids to hide their dirty laundry somewhere in their room or under their clothes. What would happen if you never did laundry? Then read Isaiah 1:16-18 and Proverbs 28:13. What can we compare our dirty clothes to? Who "washes" the sin from our lives?

Ask heart questions.

One of my husband John's great contributions to our parenting duo is his art of the shepherding conversation. Ask questions like these to help a child (or their parent) consider their own heart: How does that person feel right now? Was that loving or unloving? Was that wise or unwise? What did you actually want at that point? (See James 4:1-2.) What kind of heart did that come from? (Was it humble? Proud? Self-centered? Truthful?) What were you feeling right then? How could you have handled or said that differently?

Fresh Ink: Resources for Vibrant Faith

- For the younger kids, read picture books like *Potato Pants* by Laurie Keller, *Lilly's Purple Plastic Purse* by Kevin Henkes, and *Enemy Pie* by Derek Munson.

- With older kids, search for videos of politicians or other leaders showing contrition and humility, admitting and apologizing for mistakes. Do the apologies always seem genuine? Or do some people just seem sorry they got caught? What makes for a heartfelt apology and repentance?

True Colors: Discussion Questions for Kids

- How can you tell when someone is really sorry?

- What's the difference between someone being sorry and someone being sorry they got caught? How can you tell the difference? (Check out 2 Corinthians 7:10-11 for clues.)

Think Ink: Contemplative Questions for Parents

- Do you hesitate to apologize to your kids? Are you afraid it under-
  mines your authority or dilutes your kids' responsibility?

- How was (or wasn't) confession modeled in your home of origin?
  Whose humility and repentance do you want to model?

- Think about the story of the woman who poured perfume over Jesus's
  feet in the presence of some indignant Pharisees. Jesus observes, "Her
  many sins have been forgiven—as her great love has shown. But
  whoever has been forgiven little loves little" (Luke 7:47). Consider
  whether this woman sinned more than the Pharisees. What effects of
  confession in her life do you want to absorb?

I'm sure my own sin has handed my kids plenty of fodder for their future ther-
apists. But I hope they have just as many memories of me saying, "I'm sorry. Will
you forgive me?"

I know, I know. Confession can sound like not much fun. Maybe a bit like snivel-
ing. Or, depending on your background, maybe something like *Bless me, Father,
for I have sinned* rolls around in your head.

But what if it sounded more like handcuffs falling off?

Prayer of the Dependent Parent

Lord, my entire family needs your forgiveness—myself included. Have mercy on us.

Help mercy and realness about our sin to mark my family. Let this realness feed our love for you and compassion for each other. Show me how to separate my kids'—and my own—worth from our performance. Let me show my kids the side of you that loved to hang with sinners.

Many days I'm overwhelmed with the failures of my family. Remind me over and over again that you live with those who are humble and contrite—not those enamored of their own perfection.

15

Adoration

The Song That Never Ends

John and I, kids in tow, were maneuvering at a snail's pace through a Ugandan traffic jam in our trusty, high-clearance minivan. Our speakers happily trumpeted the Christmas CD my mom had sent us, and we chatted, energy high for our Christmas shopping in the city and the Christmas party of our nonprofit (which, with the barbecue and barefoot kids running around in shorts, looked more like the Fourth of July).

It was sometime after "Let It Snow" that our heads all swiveled to the driver's side, where a man was banging—hard—on the outside of our van. Never a good sign in Kampala.

That's when his partner whipped open my car door and swiftly grabbed my bag slouched at my feet. My casserole dish skidded across the pavement as I unbuckled without thinking, standing between unmoving lanes and yelling something very helpful, like "*Hey!*" He and his cronies sprinted away with my reading device, my phone, my drivers' licenses from both countries, and our house keys.

I make it sound lighthearted. But really I started sobbing, hands shaking, which probably frightened my children just as much as the stranger flinging open the car door. John sat quietly reeling in horror and anger: "I should have locked the doors. Why didn't I lock the doors?" Passengers around us oh-so-helpfully mimed, *You have to lock your doors in Kampala. Like this.*

The highlight of my day took place about 17 seconds after that lowlight. My then eleven-year-old spoke up: "Guys, it looks like Mom is upset right now. Let's pray." John took the cue, thanking God for the protection of our bodies and for God's control and then praying for the thieves themselves. Prayer was a gift of God in the middle of a liquid, pulsing fear. Throughout Scripture, God follows up "Do not be afraid" with his best reason: *for I am with you.* And my son had a moment of Godwardness when we all needed it most.

A friend e-mailed me later: "The very thing we would protect our children from experiencing may be the very thing that God wants to use in their lives now so that when they are adults, they'll know how to respond to crisis."[1]

God gives and takes away (here he used the latter to offer us a gift), and we can sing Christmas carols with full hearts afterward. Sometimes people wonder why God allows bad things to happen to good people—of course we, as missionaries, would be the good people in that scenario, right? But from dust I came, and hell I deserve (not "good things").

Adoration is not only what God deserves. It's God's gift to *us.*

When You're the Lucky Dog

When I look at my teenage daughter, I see a keen mind, a generous heart, and a magnet for those who are sometimes unseen. People tend to adore her. As I type, the same boy has asked her five times to the school dance. I have witnessed her making friends with kids in poverty because they're just kids to her. Or putting out a donation cup for the pregnancy center at her lemonade stand.

Someday in the future, I can see my arms crossed before some peach-fuzz-garnished guy who wants to take her out.

I see myself thinking, *You have no clue what you're getting. You think she's a pretty face and a great dancer. You may come back to take her out when you understand what a lucky dog you are.*

As the saying goes, Guns don't kill people. Parents with pretty daughters kill people. (Yes, I am messing with you.)

Some things hold such exquisite value that the intrinsic, overwhelming reward goes to the one who will mine it. There are other phenomena like this in the universe—things that leave us the losers if we miss out on appreciating them. They're things in the "Look, kids! Quick!" category.

I was scrambling for my cell phone one morning when a newborn fawn tottered through our lawn.

Effervescent me, to my teen: "You have to come see this!"

Grumpy teen: "No. I don't."

And he didn't. But he's also the one who missed out on the view of nature by choice.

C.S. Lewis speaks of artwork (or daughters) that warrants our sheer wonder—because if not,

> we shall be stupid, insensible, and great losers, we shall have missed something...[God] is that Object to admire which...is simply to be awake, to have entered the real world; not to appreciate which is to have lost the greatest experience, and in the end to have lost all...
>
> But, of course, this is not all. God does not only "demand" praise as the supremely beautiful and all-satisfying Object. He does apparently command it as lawgiver.[2]

Too often, adoration slumps toward a have-to. But sometimes I get a glimpse that it is a *get-to*. This is our breathtaking birthright, our gracious choice: to love back. We are the lucky dogs.

Praise: The Song That Never Ends

Perhaps adoration—loving God back—is easier than you'd think. Would your kids believe you if you said eating a grilled cheese could praise God? If Romans 12:1

is true, then it's all his: "Offer your bodies as a living sacrifice, holy and pleasing to God—this is your true and proper worship." Even when you burn the sandwich.

When we think *worship*, we typically think of an event, of something we start and stop and then go on our way. But the Bible has a different idea. Colossians puts it this way:

> Let the word of Christ dwell in you richly, teaching and admonishing one another in all wisdom, singing psalms and hymns and spiritual songs, with thankfulness in your hearts to God. And whatever you do, in word or deed, do everything in the name of the Lord Jesus, giving thanks to God the Father through him (3:16-17 ESV).

That means whether kids are dangling from a rope swing, screaming like a banshee, or muscling through a pop quiz—or (yep) going to the bathroom—everything is either toward God or not.

We are always worshipping something. *Because we were made for it.* God speaks of "everyone who is called by my name, whom I created for my glory...the people I formed for myself that they may proclaim my praise" (Isaiah 43:7,21). To the woman at the well, Jesus affirms, "The true worshipers will worship the Father in spirit and truth, for the Father is seeking such people to worship him" (John 4:23 ESV). And Romans 11:36 sings, "From him and through him and for him are all things. To him be the glory forever!"

Practicing adoration preps our kids' lives to be one long, seamless song toward God. More than their future career, the lives they'll touch, or the person they'll marry, they were made for *this*. To do *this*. Rather than an event, praise is a continual upward-facing lifestyle lived for God's honor and purpose—from the inside out.

By helping our kids see the stuff of their lives as open doors to adoration, we help them answer, *Who's getting the honor right now, if I'm honest? What does it look like to worship God in my work? My rest? My play?*

Oh, *There* He Is

Use your kids' strengths and interests as arrows pointing them to the way they

Permanent Truth

Adoration is about celebrating, appreciating, and enjoying God for all he is, acknowledging that his glory is the rightful center of everything. It is

- our foremost response to God

- adoring, even when others would call it a waste of time

- setting aside our flurry of effort and productivity to simply revel in God

- saying, "God, you're like my Disney World. My ice cream. My movie marathon."

- encouraging kids' strengths and interests as arrows, pointing them to the ways they feel God's pleasure

- trusting God and acknowledging him as lovingly and capably in charge, even when we're hurting and don't understand

- using gratitude to live in constant awareness of God's goodness to us, of the gifts constantly piling up around us, even in hard times

- lifting our eyes from our own belly buttons into worship, trust, and joy

- drawing a dotted line from every gift back to the Giver

feel God's pleasure. Are they bookworms? Athletes? Artists? Building enthusiasts? Baby-doll nurturers? Experts at styling hair? How can they use these skills for God's pleasure?

Check out what God says of a man named Bezalel in the time when the Israelites were constructing the tabernacle:

> The LORD said to Moses, "See, I have called by name Bezalel...I have filled him with the Spirit of God, with ability and intelligence, with knowledge and all craftsmanship, to devise artistic designs, to work in gold, silver, and bronze, in cutting stones for setting, and in carving wood, to work in every craft. And behold, I have appointed with him Oholiab...And I have given to all able men ability, that they may make all that I have commanded you" (Exodus 31:1-6 ESV).

How has God gifted your kids to reveal him as beautiful? Help your kids see that their enjoyment and gifting are from him and for him, even when their work is not distinctly "Christian." Excellence in completing math homework or emptying the dishwasher pleases God too—not just because we're humming a praise song. God cares about how we work. In fact, the Hebrew word *avodah* was used in the Old Testament to jointly mean "work" and "worship" and "service."

Talk to your kids about how you sense God's happiness about the way you're made, whether it's in your occupation, fixing things around your house, or changing diapers. Show your kids that they can praise God with their work and unique contributions, even in the most mundane acts of faithful, regular life.

Gratitude: A Lifestyle of Kindness Hunting

It was one of those weeks when the phrase from the Morton Salt box from my childhood had to be occasionally batted from my mind: *When it rains, it pours.*

It started on the way to the airport, where John would fly from Uganda to Kenya for two weeks. Neither of our ATM cards were working, which is problematic in a nation that functions nearly entirely on cash. Of course, it wasn't until paying for my parking that I realized I didn't even have the 80 cents to make it out of the parking lot. I commissioned the kids to look under all the car mats and in the cup holders. Still 40 cents shy. I had to ask for a handout from someone else.

The next day (after our family thankfully not spending the night in the car park), my son was hit on his bike by a motorcycle; the driver, looking nervous, had carried him to our door.

Liberally sprinkle in some hormones (those would be mine), mix vigorously with three rowdy boys without their father there to wrestle them to the ground, marinate in intermittent water and power, and it was a recipe for one of those weeks when a girl resorts to Lamaze breathing. Of course, one of us would be hit by a motorcycle taxi this week.

But part of the beauty, honestly, was living that week in Africa.

It's hard to complain about having to bum gas money from a friend when I have a car and a cash source—once we get that pesky card issue straightened out. (About .8 percent of Ugandans own a vehicle.) It's hard to be disgruntled about kid-wrangling on my own when: a) John is serving God doing something he's incredible at, and b) Uganda is flooded with single moms who have no rescuer scheduled for arrival in a week and a half. It's hard to make a big deal of being without electricity, considering only 15 percent of the country is wired for it. It's hard to make too much of my son walking away from his accident with an injured arm, in light of the five deaths per day from motorbikes in the capital city alone, or the taxi-related injuries that make up 40 percent of trauma cases at the main hospital.[3]

Africa has marked me. It has not altered me in a way that most people who see me will ever witness, though the difference is almost bodily. It's as if I've had eye surgery, and the world will never enter my brain the same. Its mark is indelible now on my decisions, my perspective.

In brain scans, happiness is nearly indistinguishable from gratitude.[4] And that gratitude helps combat anxiety and depression because, as evidence suggests, "gratitude and anxiety are mutually exclusive neural pathways."[5]

Admittedly, gratitude is not always easy. I shove some events into the category of "I want to forget" instead of training my eyes to find God in all that happened. But there's still value—spirituality included—to be had in my honesty that some weeks are discouraging, angering, and painful. (Novelist Elizabeth Berg reminds me, "The person with the bleeding finger doesn't hurt less for the person next to him with the bleeding arm."[6]) Dishonesty about loss and pain doesn't liberate us (see John 8:32). But perspective and gratitude? That week, they just might have set me free. It's a way we all long for our kids to be free too.

Writing on the Wall: Practical Ideas

Try prayers where you simply admire God and call him by his names.

"God, you are El Shaddai, 'God Almighty.'" Or, as characters in the Bible have done, describe what he has been to you lately: "You're my best friend."

Keep a running list of what your family is thankful for.

At dinner each night for a month, see if your family can name ten more things they are thankful for. You can do this during errands too: *Ten things we're thankful for. Go.*

Create a thankfulness tablecloth.

For dinner one night, use craft paper as a tablecloth. Lay out markers or crayons to cover it with what you're thankful for.

Share thanksgiving notes.

Drop a small note in your son, daughter, or husband's lunch, or put a sticky note where they'll find it at just the right time. "When I think of what I'm thankful for, you always come to mind. I love you." Or "Thanks for the ways you _____. I love you so much."

Help your kids record a video "greeting card" for a relative far away.

Have them describe their appreciation for that person's influence in their lives. (Let them get creative with the props.) Or roll out the butcher paper to design a banner you'll send in the mail as a special surprise.

Make a gratitude poster.

On the back of an interior door, fasten a piece of poster board and keep a pen attached. Make it a family goal to fill the poster board with objects of your gratitude. Alternatively, utilize Ann Voskamp's idea of covering a window with sticky notes of gratitude.[7]

Use calmness to worship.

Stretch on the floor together, relaxing and praying before bedtime. As you inhale, thank God for something specific; as you exhale, praise him for one of his names or characteristics. When my kids are anxious, I'm amazed at how rapidly this activity calms them.

Set aside times for nature wonder.

Wake up your kids for a meteor shower or eclipse. Or pull over for that scenic overlook. Or pack a picnic lunch, letting the kids hunt for the perfect spot. Gather flowers or the most striking fallen leaves. Even science homework is a way to marvel over God's baffling genius. Talk together about your observations, and gently direct things Godward. Reflect in silence.

Huddle for a quick morning prayer.

Sure, you can ask God for a good day, but the ultimate idea? *This day, God, is for you.* When they get home, thank God together for good things when you're talking about their day, or maybe just observe, "That's great! I'm so thankful for that!" "Hey, answered prayer! Cool!" (Fist bump.) As you create touch points for your kids throughout the day, pointing them back to God, your praise becomes more and more contiguous.

Gather gel pens or markers and index cards for times of devotion or during sermons.

Let your kids write and illuminate verses of Scripture, characteristics of God they love, or thoughts they want to remember. The cards can be posted in rooms or inside closets or cupboards, used as bookmarks, taped on mirrors, or tucked into backpacks or lunches as reminders.

Help your kids create a worship playlist.

This can help them pray and worship God during the week, perhaps using different tracks for getting ready in the morning, studying, and working out. You might listen together and purchase new songs to generate excitement and unique enthusiasm for worship. Help them see that their style could be different from the style of worship at your church.

Create warm memories around worship times at church.

Hug them. Smile at them. Wrap your arms around them while you sing.

Have the kids create a haiku.

This is the part of the book where you might chalk me up as a nutter. But try this: Show your kids how to create a haiku to express themselves to God. For all of you feeling a little rusty on your poetry, a haiku is a three-line poem: one line of five syllables, then another of seven syllables, then a final line of five. For example:

> *Intimacy mine*
> *whispered favor, head on chest*
> *Can you hear? He's there.*

Play a musical instrument.

I have had a few cool moments with my kids tucked beside me at the piano, singing worship songs they picked. How can you use your strengths to point your kids upward?

Remind kids to prepare their hearts for worship.

This could be like the Hebrews did after sunset on Friday nights, or the day before in their Day of Preparation. Before church, you might play worship music as your family gets ready (better than fighting, right?). On the way to church, consider talking about what you're thankful for that week.

Teach your kids about intercessory worship.

For me, this means taking a song and turning it into a prayer for someone on my mind. You can pray for countries or choose to praise God amid something hard. Maybe at night before bed, when your kids are talking about someone they're concerned about, help them choose a song they want to "pray" for that person. Music is emotionally moving, so these may feel like intimate, vibrant prayers.

Focus on gratitude as a family.

Set a goal of five minutes each day.

Train your eyes to "see."

Seek to genuinely thank every person, looking them in the eye: the gas station attendant, the cashier, the server, the janitor, the Sunday school teacher—and your kiddos for the giddy joy they bring you.

Keep a list of the little reminders that God is walking with you.

Going through a heart-wrenching season? Will's gratitude during his cancer scare inspired us to write on a neon-yellow index card a working list of all the little reminders that God was walking with us—all the small graces he was handing us mixed up in this sorrow. I still keep it tucked in a journal. Keep a list of your own to remember that God is for you (see Romans 8:31).

Use visual cues to help you think in new ways about gratitude.

A tube of toothpaste might prompt a quick prayer of thanks for good dental care; pulling out of the driveway, for a peaceful street and quality roads; the receipt at a restaurant, for a wholesome meal and washed dishes and the finances to pay for it. Thank God out loud with your kids as you leave the grocery store with enough food and as you fill the tank with gas.

Give kids the gift of hard work.

In a culture where everyone gets a ribbon and the norm is to hand our kids what they want, entitlement needs an equally powerful antidote. Give your kids the opportunity to work for what they want, and to work as part of being a family. This develops in kids a hard-earned appreciation for what arrives in their hands.

Plant a garden or a few vegetable-bearing plants.

Most kids don't understand the amount of effort that goes into the piles of produce at the supermarket. Guide them toward gratitude for what we consume.

Memorize Scripture passages about gratitude (small rewards may help).

Some to try: Psalm 100; 16:5-11; 1 Thessalonians 5:16-18.

Fresh Ink: Resources for Vibrant Faith

- Using a large sheet of paper and markers for each child, walk together through Rick Warren's SHAPE acronym to help them discover the unique ways God's sculpted them and their story for his honor. Help kids see in each component a way they're uniquely designed to worship him.
- Help older kids discover their "Sacred Pathways." Search for author Gary Thomas's various ways that we each best connect with God—like our own worship "personality." Maybe that's not surprising as you begin to uncover your occupation and personal makeup as an avenue for worship. (I've got at least one activist and one caregiver.) Encourage them to try out other pathways that intrigue them.
- Download FamilyLife's free gratitude activities, like a gratitude scavenger hunt, at familylife.com/family-gratitude-plan/.
- We've loved these picture books for teaching generosity and gratitude:

  - *Those Shoes* by Maribeth Boelts

- *Boxes for Katje* by Candace Fleming
- *The Orange Shoes* by Trinka Hakes Noble
- *Beatrice's Goat* by Page McBrier
- *The All-I'll-Ever-Want Christmas Doll* by Patricia McKissack
- *The Firefighters' Thanksgiving* by Maribeth Boelts
- At janelbreitenstein.com/permanentmarkers/adoration, find free printable thank-you notes for kids and 62 things to be grateful for if you live in the developed world.

True Colors: Discussion Questions for Kids

- Worshipping God doesn't seem to be something a lot of people think is important. Do you? Why? Have you ever done something good and no one noticed? What if someone did something for you that was hard or amazing, but you didn't say thank you?

- Remember when we saw…? [Insert amazing nature event or spectacle: an eclipse, a visit to the Grand Canyon, etc.] What if we had missed out on that? Who would have been the "losers"?

- What's the difference between whining or complaining and telling the truth about something hard that's going on?

- What things do we often take for granted but should be thankful for?

Think Ink: Contemplative Questions for Parents

- What gifts do you attribute to your own hard work, excellence, or character? Consider praying, *Show my heart how everything I have has been received (1 Corinthians 4:7). Help me believe it.*

- Reflect on gifts you received even before your lifetime. When you trace the good things you enjoy through generations, whose decisions and life circumstances also flow into yours? Whose metaphorical shoulders do you stand on? How would your life differ if those before you had made alternate life choices (e.g., not to emigrate, not to follow God, not to value having children)?

- Is personal time to adore God a priority to you? Why or why not?

I spend loads of money and oodles of time in the hopes that my kids get to do what they were made to do—and clearly, occupation is a big part of that. But even more than becoming a graphic artist or a Marine, my kids were made to worship God.

If life finds them in a wheelchair, with an autoimmune disorder, in a painful marriage, or flipping burgers when I thought they'd make good math teachers, they can still adore God and fulfill every purpose for which they were designed.

Prayer of the Dependent Parent

Lord, culture makes it so much easier for my family to feel entitled rather than grateful. Show us specific ways to combat that entitlement, and expose to me my kids' true attitudes—even while I'm trusting you to change them.

We are naturally always worshipping something—but I confess it is not naturally you. As John Calvin said, our hearts are "idol-making factories." Help me to lead in seeing and adoring you for who you are. Show me what stands in the way of seeing you as you are (1 John 3:1-3).

For us, I pray Paul's prayer for the Ephesians: that the eyes of our hearts may be enlightened so we may know the hope to which you've called us, the riches of your glorious inheritance in your holy people, and your incomparably great power for us who believe (Ephesians 1:18-19).

Wake us up to worship, Lord.

"Lord, it is fitting to rejoice in your beauty and to gaze upon your handiwork. While others may call this a waste of time, we recognize that unless we sit in adoration of you, we will forget whom we serve and for what purpose. Remind us why worship is always our first response to you. Amen." [8]

16

Celebrating the Wins

In my dad's garage are stashed a few items that would be of little significance to anyone else but that mean the world to him. One of them is a charred license plate.

"This," he's told me, "represents the day God saved me and my family."

The blackened license plate was removed from a 1977 Cadillac Seville. The driver was my youthful mother, heavily pregnant with me, her firstborn. Only a half mile from our farmhouse, she'd yielded at the intersection. But it was summer. The field of Midwest corn stretched green and high. Another car was charging through, somewhere around the posted 55 miles per hour.

The impact sent her car into the opposite field. Stunned but still the steady, keen-thinking mom I would come to know, she heaved from the car both herself and a friend's foster infant she'd been watching.

When she stepped away, the car exploded in flames.

"In that moment," my dad told me, "God saved my whole family."

He explained that the Israelites made a monument to remind themselves of the miracle God accomplished in their midst, guiding them through the rippling Jordan on dry ground. Each tribe selected a large stone to contribute: "When your children ask in time to come, 'What do those stones mean to you?' then you shall tell them that the waters of the Jordan were cut off before the ark of the covenant of the Lord…So these stones shall be to the people of Israel a memorial forever" (Joshua 4:6-7 esv).

A license plate. This is one of my family's monuments.

Some days of parenting hit us at 55 miles per hour, spinning us around, leaving us bruised. Some flay us open, making us bloody and bewildered. And yet, God can't seem to help himself—he constantly creates small and large acts of salvation in us and our kids.

These moments—even those that leave us limping—we need to keep.

Like when John turns to me at night and relays evidence that our son's heart is changing. Or when I opened an e-mail telling of a scholarship to a writer's conference, in which God seemed to whisper, *You have a future and a purpose here too.* Or licking coconut cream pie and chili from my lips at my in-laws' after John baptized two of our kids. Or thumbing through journal entries—some with exclamation points, some with small, round water stains—both of which remind me that Jesus Christ is the same yesterday, today, and forever (Hebrews 13:8).

For in all the stones (or license plates) we collect in parenting, "who is a rock, except our God?" (Psalm 18:31 esv). My "faith stones" bring to mind a Zulu song roughly translated, "God, you have walked with us this whole way."

So let's train our eyes to see God working steadily around us, from the child who remembers to say thank you—or flush the toilet—to the painstakingly slow ways God is changing our kids in seasons where our heart twists like a dishrag. After all, "the eye is the lamp of the body. So, if your eye is healthy, your whole body will be full of light" (Matthew 6:22 esv).

Let's be wakeful and present to God's activity among us, like Moses asking God to show his glory.

I welcome your love for my kids and for me. I acknowledge this is from you, that every good and perfect gift I enjoy comes from a good God (James 1:17). Your power is here and breathtaking.

This is what we celebrate as parents. What we remember. Because loss never gets the last word in the Bible.

God does.

Prayer of the Dependent Parent

Lord, I need the eyes of my heart enlightened (Ephesians 1:18). I want to see you, to see your glory. I want to show that glory to my kids and celebrate all the ways we see you working around us. Let us cultivate fun and gratitude and delight because we're your kids.

I believe you complete every good work you begin (Philippians 1:6). Show me how to work alongside you effectively to raise these kids—and to leave the results in your hands. Be welcomed, famed, and remembered in my family until we can ultimately celebrate with you forever.

———————

Group Discussion Guide

Introduction
The Need to Know

1. How would you articulate goals you have for your kids, small and not-so-much?

2. Which more minor goals tend to sap energy, intentionality, and time from your more major, eternal goals? What practical steps might be necessary for change?

3. The author quotes Dave Harvey's words about deterministic, legalistic parenting. How does your gut respond to God being in charge of our kids' growth (1 Corinthians 3:6)? Talk about the tension between our agency as parents—what we can and should affect—and God's control over kids' hearts.

4. How do you sense your identity being intertwined with your kids' success? In what ways, in the words of Reb Bradley, do you sense your temptation to effectively trade your children's hearts for your reputation?

5. Talk about the differences in current (and past) spiritual responsiveness of each of your kids, and how this influences the way you disciple them.

6. How did you experience the power of "catching the bug" of something in your childhood? Who portrayed Christ or spiritual growth as compelling to you—and how did they do it, even if you came to Christ as an adult?

Chapter 1
Identity: Who Do You Think You Are?

1. With which of Nouwen's three lies or Keller's idols do you most regularly identify? What temptations toward a false identity—one outside of Jesus—are most alluring to you?

2. How do you witness the interplay between pride and insecurity in yourself and your kids?

3. Which "soul holes" do you suspect might most strongly influence each of your children? (Consider this an ongoing investigation.)

4. How would the gospel, the "shame-antidote," address your kids' pet idols?

5. Which of the ideas in this chapter inspire you to action? What's one way you'll parent your kids differently in the area of identity?

Chapter 2
Prayer: Listening Up

1. What's one desire you have for your family's prayer life?

2. Who or what has been influential in teaching you to pray?

3. From this chapter's "Think Ink: Contemplative Questions for Parents," share adjectives that describe your prayer life. Share times, too, when you've felt either frustrated in prayer or encouraged by your interactions with God. What emotions or disappointments do you associate with prayer? What desires to you have for your own prayer life?

4. What techniques have boosted your own prayer life? Perhaps in a different angle, what ways have you found it helpful to feel connected to God?

5. What is your family's (or your own) most felt obstacle to the prayer life you'd like to experience? What's one practical idea you'd like to implement toward that end?

Chapter 3
Self-Control: The Power of What We Don't Do

1. We're frequently encouraged to "just be yourself." But in light of this chapter's introduction, what are some issues you see with that philosophy?

2. What's the difference between placating a child and avoiding circumstances where they're less likely to lose control? When might it be necessary for a child to continue in an environment where they could emotionally lose control?

3. If we're seeking to help kids "feel and deal" by modeling, what's the place of a parent's emotions? In your mind, to what extent should a parent restrain emotion, and when shouldn't they?

4. How does a lack of self-control typically manifest itself in each of your kids?

5. Under what "perfect storms" are your kids (and yourself) most likely to lack self-control? What's one practical measure you'd like to implement or plan in advance for these situations?

6. How did your home of origin deal with strong emotions? How has this influenced how you deal with those?

7. As you consider those situations, what idols/identity "holes" likely lie beneath that lack of self-control? Could it be fear or anxiety? A desire for approval, power, or security?

8. What's one unhealthy emotional response pattern of your own which you can target?

Chapter 4
Meditation: On Keeping Quiet

1. What are natural breaks in your schedule that might allow for "nothing time" for you or your kids, to lead to more times of meditation? (It might be driving to work, after-school time, Sunday afternoons, or after dinner.)

2. Which of your kids is more naturally contemplative? More naturally busy and activity-oriented?

3. What aptitudes of your kids could serve as avenues to contemplation and meditation (the author mentions science, music, art, dance, politics...)?

4. Do you personally tend to read (and likely model) Scripture for information or transformation? What helps you personally respond to what you're reading with life change?

5. What are personally your most effective ways to help Scripture saturate you? Do you journal? Talk with a friend? Wrestle with God? If this isn't a strength of yours, where does the breakdown usually occur?

6. The author mentions, "The noise in my life chokes out God's presence in my life and affects my ability to listen" (page 72). This is reminiscent of Joyce Huggett: "In the stillness we can shed some of the pressures which would prevent us receiving God's Word into the innermost core of our being."[1] How are your experiences with God different when they're unrushed? How are you different?

7. What activities—even those for God, and even in your devotional times—might be distracting you from knowing God and being with him?

Chapter 5
Studying God's Word: Learning to Feed Ourselves

1. How have you learned the Bible most potently and engagingly? What are your hopes for your kids' Bible knowledge, understanding, and love?

2. The Pharisees elevated Scripture and sought to obey even its tiniest points—like tithing their spices (Matthew 23:23). The author points out that the Pharisees' stringent, man-made rules kept them from seeking God's heart and application in every circumstance. Jesus tells them, "You have taken away the key to knowledge" (Luke 11:52). How do you think it happens that the very tool for knowing God— his Word—becomes an obstacle to that end?

3. What strengths and weaknesses would you guess your child gleans from your attitude toward God's Word?

4. Who do you tend to see as those best equipped or most responsible for your child's discipleship? Who do you see as your kids' ultimate spiritual education coordinators? Explain your thoughts.

5. When you're honest, what are your most compelling reasons for your kids to know the Bible?

6. What's one way you could share with the group that's helped your kids study God's Word? Are there any new methods—from your group or this book—you hope to add to your repertoire of ideas?

Chapter 6
Simplicity: When Less Is So Much More

1. What areas of your family's life feel harried? What values do those express? Are those receiving an appropriate priority level?

2. The author observes that "the amassing of wealth and possessions seems to be as American as apple pie" (page 98). In your words, how would your own culture answer, "If you ___, your life will sing" (page 98)?

3. "While I like to think I'm clear-eyed about the emptiness of worldly gain, sometimes my view of God's favor—of being '#blessed'—can be very prescriptive. Sometimes it's a thinly veiled version of the American dream" (page 98). Looking at the life stories of Mary, John the Baptist, Jesus, and others favored by God, how do you think we sometimes get God's favor wrong?

4. Allow for a weird illustration, if you would. Have you ever heard of a cowbird? It lays its eggs in other birds' nests. The birds doing the actual feeding and parenting don't usually differentiate between feeding the cowbird and their own nestlings. But the baby cowbirds chirp louder for food, and grow faster and larger—to the point that some of the host bird's nestlings may not survive. What in your life chirps for your attention and energy, sometimes robbing the true nurture of your kids and their souls?

5. In your words, what are the purposes of fasting and simplicity? Why do we resist them? How could these uncomfortable, inconvenient life skills become compelling?

6. In discussing these life skills, what's one aspect of life you'd like to simplify for a higher purpose?

Chapter 7
Holy Sexuality: We Are Worth More Than This

1. As a kid, what or who were your sources of information about sex? How was that good or bad?

2. What fears influence (or at least nag) you about your kids and sex? About these conversations? What personal obstacles make this challenging?

3. Talk about your opinions of Dr. Juli Slattery's perspective on sexual purity versus sexual integrity (page 119).

4. Describe the relationship you hope to have with your kids regarding talks like this. How would you describe your mental list of "How to Deal: What I Believe About Awkward, Hairy Topics with Children" (page 111)?

Chapter 8
Community: Almost Home

1. The author relates, "Isolation honestly felt safer than needing others, than exposing myself to judgment or rejection or misunderstanding" (page 132). How does isolation manage to feel both safer and more shameful? What are some of the fears and pain that compound themselves in isolation?

2. How have you seen a cultural shift to isolation and away from community over your lifetime?

3. How does Jesus's change of our identity (see chapter 1) set us free for true community?

4. How does our culture—not to mention our sin—distort the purposes of hospitality?

5. What's most daunting or difficult about hospitality for you and your family? What's one practical way you could move toward others in hospitality, practically and with courage?

6. Who do you know that truly listens and makes people feel at home even outside of the context of a house? How do they demonstrate presence with others?

Chapter 9
Discernment: Sorting the Skittles

1. Describe a situation in your life when someone overwhelmed you with undeserved kindness—a picture of God's grace. How does our own experience with mercy and God's compassion influence discernment?

2. What practical methods do you use to discern kids' media—and help them begin to discern media on their own?

3. Look up Luke 20:1-8. How does Jesus respond to the Pharisees' manipulation? Why doesn't he give them more truth about himself?

4. How do you personally discern between the Holy Spirit's voice and your own inclinations? What are you most likely to mistake for the Holy Spirit?

5. What spiritual practices or circumstances help you shut out the "noise" around you and allow Scripture and your knowledge of God to inform your decisions?

Chapter 10
Service: Downward Mobility

1. Describe one of the most meaningful ways someone has served you or your family. What does your experience tell you about what's significant to others?

2. Looking at your individual kids' design, what ways do you imagine you could connect their gifts and interests with service?

3. When you think about this life skill, what emotions are immediate? Inspired? Overwhelmed? Guilty? Exhausted? Resentful (for ways you've served resulting in burnout or other negative experiences)?

4. What do you want to pass on to your kids from your own experiences in service? What do you want to improve or avoid?

5. What are the most daunting or frustrating snags that keep your family from serving? What's one doable way you could create space to develop a family culture of seeing and serving?

Chapter 11
Sharing our Faith: Loving Them This Much

1. This chapter's potentially controversial. Why is evangelism so offensive in our culture? Is it more than the "foolishness" of the cross (1 Corinthians 1:23)?

2. Aside from the clear awakening of the Holy Spirit, what circumstances and techniques have you seen effective in reaching the next generation with faith?

3. As you feel comfortable, talk about how you came to Christ. What was happening within you and around you? What conversations or relationships worked their way into your soul?

4. "Day after day, the best and truest evangelism seems to be accomplished by *great lovers of people and lovers of God*. A lack of evangelism—a horizontal issue—may be an indicator of a vertical problem: a lack of a lively, leafy relationship with God" (page 173). What are some of your greatest hurdles to sharing your faith?

5. This chapter's strategies largely center around hearing someone's story—where they've come from; their questions, pain, and shame. What questions do you find helpful to begin or continue meaningful, Godward conversations?

Chapter 12
Resilience: Your Child, Stronger

1. Baby Boomers and Gen Xers may remember more of a "free-range" childhood than younger generations—less supervised, more independent. What cultural shifts have led to more vigilant (some have argued coddling) childhood experiences? Talk about the pros and cons of both.

2. Recount a childhood experience or consistent weakness that taught you resilience. How did your home of origin handle grief and other negative emotions? Which of these do you want to perpetuate in your home—and which do you want to revamp?

3. Where does your own parenting fall on the spectrum of control versus independence of your kids? If you're married, describe the differences between yourself and your spouse.

4. The North American spiritual narrative can often be one of increased success and happiness as we move further into faith. But the author quotes Father Thomas Keating: "The spiritual journey is not a career or a success story. It is a series of small humiliations of the false self that become more and more profound" (see page 190). Consider the lives of devoted Christians in the Bible. Discuss how resilience and grief can prepare our kids for a genuine, fire-tested lifetime of faith.

5. With each of your own kids (and without betraying a confidence), what weaknesses or setbacks has God "gifted" them with—and how are they personally responding? Practically speaking, how do you hope to shape their resilience?

Chapter 13
Respecting Authority: Stepping Down

1. Which of your kids is more naturally compliant? More rebellious? What can be some of the hidden hazards of parenting both?

2. How did your family of origin handle obedience? What do you hope to replicate, and what do you want to do differently?

3. What's one of your strengths in parenting for obedience? On the flip side, what's its weakness?

4. What's most discouraging to you as you try to teach obedience?

5. Culturally, many of us are more emotionally intelligent parents than generations before us. But the gap between an authority figure and a child is also closing, for better and worse. How do you personally navigate the tension between maintaining authority over your kids while pursuing connection and attachment?

Chapter 14
Confession and Repentance: Regrets Only

1. As you feel comfortable (and without betraying a confidence), describe a personal experience when forgiveness altered circumstances in a significant way.

2. This chapter talks about creating a family culture and lifestyle of repentance and forgiveness. Who in your life (if anyone) has modeled this kind of humility?

3. What's the difference between frequently apologizing and overapologizing (i.e. "sorry" as a shield from anger or criticism)?

4. What keeps us as parents from apologizing to our kids?

Chapter 15
Adoration: The Song That Never Ends

1. Considering your kids' natural interests and talents, what are ways you could connect those to worship and enjoyment of God? What does this look like in your own life?

2. Martin Luther reputedly said, "The maid who sweeps her kitchen is doing the will of God just as much as the monk who prays—not because she may sing a Christian hymn as she sweeps but because God loves clean floors." How do you experience God in your vocation and life's dailiness?

3. When—and doing what—have you felt closest to and most naturally worshipful of God?

4. The author describes a week when, in spite of her son's motorcycle accident, perspective carried her to gratitude. Describe a time in your own life when perspective has compelled you to thankfulness.

5. Why, in your words, are worship and gratitude worth our time and the time of our kids?

6. What's one feasible way you could see yourself drawing your family into more worship and gratitude?

Acknowledgments

The more I write, the more God whisks up in me a thankfulness for his body, for the community that writes a book, though the keyboard is tapped by one primary person. I remain grateful for all the people God gifted to think of what I didn't, observe what I spaced, and redline what I definitely should not say.

Thank you to Dan Balow, the first agent to see me as having something to say. Thank you, Bob Hostetler, agent extraordinaire, for helping me shape an idea into a concept that could love a reader well.

To the crackerjack team at Harvest House—particularly my adored editor, Kathleen Kerr—and certainly Andy Rogers, Shari MacDonald Strong, and Kim Tanner: Thank you for spending your expertise to shape and launch this message. Thank you too for your vision on behalf of other families who are just trying to get rowdy kids to wear underwear and put two of the same shoes on the correct feet.

Rebecca Price, this book (and most of my career) wouldn't have existed without your mentorship, long conversations over generous meals, and friendship that surprised both of us. Thank you, friend, for never letting me quit, because God's kingdom is worth our best, and often our failure.

To friends and family who cheered me on, raised a glass, and believed in this book—especially Brady and Tori, Michael and Nicole, Ryan and Melissa, Tamara Sims, and all the Breits: Thank you.

To FamilyLife, one of the first to grant me a platform—and continually so—to speak hope to families: I remain grateful for you and your heart for homes.

To Refuge and Hope International and to my son's learning disabilities, which awakened my passion for creative teaching: I am indebted to you.

My three sisters and their spouses affirmed that life could have purpose beyond Africa. They stoked courage in me, since people-pleasing and finding one's voice make terrible bedfellows.

In writing this, I stand on the shoulders of two uber-intentional parents, Gary and Cindy, who love Jesus with their lives. To watch you follow God in leave-it-all faith even when sacrifices were great—and to observe you growing in the knowledge of God into your sixties—is a gift I hope will echo for generations after me. Your generous legacy leaves enormous shoes to fill.

To my kids, whom the Holy Spirit used to form this book in me, one sticky floor, unflushed toilet, bedtime story, crash-and-burn parenting fumble, and holy moment at a time: I have no greater joy than to know my children are walking in the truth (3 John 1:4). Your stories are written together with mine, and being your mom has been one of the greatest privileges of my life. May God form you into oaks of righteousness for his honor, even if (especially if?) it takes a lot of repentance along the way. You make me deeply happy.

John: This book is as much yours as mine. To paraphrase Neruda, I lose track of where you end and I begin. Since we met, you've constantly seen more of God's vision for me than I have, even with all my wild ideas. I lose track of how many times a day I thank him for you—and who you've shaped me to be with your gentle lion of a heart; your patient, relentless shepherding of us; your outright hilarity; and your brilliant, fertile mind. Thank you for advocating for me when courage and vision had fled. Our love story could only be God's idea.

To the Author of every life story: "All that we have accomplished you have done for us" (Isaiah 26:12). There aren't enough words in the universe to give what you're due. So "not to us, Lord, not to us but to your name be the glory, because of your love and faithfulness" (Psalm 115:1).

Notes

Foreword

1. Eric E. Peterson, preface to *Run with the Horses: The Quest for Life at Its Best*, by Eugene H. Peterson (Downers Grove, IL: InterVarsity Press, 2019), 2.

Introduction—The Need to Know

1. Dave Harvey, "Lift the Heavy Burden of Shame: How to Care for Parents of Prodigals," Desiring God, August 21, 2017, https://www.desiringgod.org/articles/lift-the-heavy -burden-of-shame.

2. Reb Bradley, "Exposing Major Blind Spots..." *Oklahoma Christian Educators Consociation*, Fall 2013. As reprinted in "Exposing Major Blind Spots of Homeschoolers by Reb Bradley." Springs of Grace Church, September 20, 2011, https://springsofgrace .church/2011/09/exposing-major-blind-spots-of-homeschoolers-by-reb-bradley/; emphasis added.

3. Ibid.

4. James K.A. Smith, *You Are What You Love,* Grand Rapids, Brazos Press, 2016), 37.

Chapter 1—Identity: Who Do You Think You Are?

1. Henri Nouwen, *Spiritual Direction: Wisdom for the Long Walk of Faith* (New York: HarperCollins, 2006), 28-29.

2. Paul David Tripp, *Parenting: 14 Gospel Principles That Can Radically Change Your Family* (Wheaton, IL: Crossway, 2016), 77.

3. C.S. Lewis, "The Weight of Glory," June 8, 1942, Wheelersburg Local School District, http://www.wheelersburg.net/Downloads/Lewis%20Glory.pdf.

4. Adapted from John Owen, as quoted in Timothy Keller, *Prayer: Experiencing Awe and Intimacy with God* (New York: Dutton, 2014): "A minister may fill his pews, his communion roll, the mouths of the public, but what that minister is on his knees in secret before God Almighty, that he is and no more."

5. Concept featured in Timothy Keller, *The Freedom of Self-Forgetfulness: The Path to True Christian Joy* (LaGrange, KY: 10Publishing, 2012).

6. Heather Davis Nelson, "10 Things You Should Know about Shame," Crossway.com, June 20, 2016, https://www.crossway.org/blog/2016/06/10-things-you-should-know -about-shame/.

7. Jamie Miller, *10-Minute Life Lessons for Kids: 52 Fun and Simple Games and Activities to Teach Your Children Honesty, Trust, Love, and Other Important Values* (New York: HarperPerennial, 1998), 48-49.

8. Bobby Schuller, "Creed of the Beloved," https://hourofpower.org/thecreedofthebeloved/.

9. Deb Heefner, personal video conversation with author, January 28, 2020.

Chapter 2—Prayer: Listening Up

1. Peter Kreeft, *Angels and Demons: What Do We Really Know About Them?* (San Francisco, CA: Ignatius Press, 1995), 23.

2. Thomas Kelly, *A Testament of Devotion* (New York: HarperCollins, 1992), 8-9.

Chapter 3—Self-Control: The Power of What We Don't Do

1. Michael Shammas, "Outrage Culture Kills Important Conversation," *HuffPost*, January 27, 2017, https://www.huffpost.com/entry/from-liberal-college-camp_b_9070894.

2. "Emotion is a primary driving force of our existence," Curt Thompson, MD, *The Soul of Shame: Retelling the Stories We Believe about Ourselves* (Downers Grove, IL: InterVarsity Press, 2015), 50.

3. Water Mischel, Ebbe B. Ebbesen, and Antonette Raskoff Zeiss, "Cognitive and Attentional Mechanisms in Delay of Gratification," *Journal of Personality and Social Psychology* 21, no. 2 (1972): 204-18, doi: 10.1037/h0032198.

4. Y. Shoda, Walter Mischel, and P.K. Peake, "Predicting Adolescent Cognitive and Self-Regulatory Competencies from Preschool Delay of Gratification: Identifying Diagnostic Conditions," *Developmental Psychology* 26, no. 6 (1990), 978-86, doi: 10.1037/0012-1649.26.6.978.

5. Tyler W. Watts, Greg J. Duncan, Haonan Quan, "Revisiting the Marshmallow Test: A Conceptual Replication Investigating Links Between Early Delay of Gratification and Later Outcomes," *Psychological Science* 29, no. 7 (July 2018), 1159-77, doi: 10.1177/0956797618761661.

6. Fred Rogers, *You Are Special: Neighborly Words of Wisdom from Mister Rogers* (New York: Penguin Books, 1995), 74.

7. D.R. Becker et al., "Behavioral Self-Regulation and Executive Function Both Predict Visuomotor Skills and Early Academic Achievement," *Early Childhood Research Quarterly* 29 (2014): 411-24, doi: 10.1016/j.ecresq.2014.04.014.

8. Michelle M. Martel et al., "Childhood and Adolescent Resiliency, Regulation, and Executive Functioning in Relation to Adolescent Problems and Competence in a High-Risk Sample," *Development and Psychopathology* 19, no. 2 (April 2007): 54-63, doi: 10.1017/S0954579407070265.

9. A.R. Sutin, L. Ferrucci, A.B. Zonderman, and A. Terracciano, "Personality and Obesity Across the Adult Life Span," *Journal of Personality and Social Psychology* 101, no. 3 (2011): 579-92, doi: 10.1037/a0024286

10. Peg Dawson and Richard Guare, *Smart but Scattered: The Revolutionary "Executive Skills" Approach to Helping Kids Reach Their Potential* (New York: Guilford, 2009), 80.

11. Catholic activist Dorothy Day said, "We have to create an environment where it is easier to be good." Quoted in Shane Claiborne, Jonathan Wilson-Hartgrove, and Enuma

Okoro, *Common Prayer: A Liturgy for Ordinary Radicals* (Grand Rapids: Zondervan, 2010), 462.

12. Jane E. Barker and Yuko Munakata, "Time Isn't of the Essence: Activating Goals Rather Than Imposing Delays Improves Inhibitory Control in Children," *Psychological Science* 26, no. 12 (December 2015): 1898-1908, doi: 10.1177/0956797615604625.

13. Michelle Anthony, "Why Impulse Control Is Harder Than Ever," *Scholastic*, https://www.scholastic.com/parents/family-life/parent-child/why-impulse-control-harder-ever.html, accessed June 4, 2020; emphasis added.

14. Paul David Tripp, "How to Be Good and Angry by Paul David Tripp," Westminster Theological Seminary, April 8, 2009, YouTube video, https://www.youtube.com/watch?v=yl0UNm6uQqE.

15. Ibid.

16. Amy Carmichael, *If: What Do I Know of Calvary Love?* (Fort Washington, PA: CLC Publications, 2011), 35.

17. Alessandro Gabbiadini et al., "Interactive Effect of Moral Disengagement and Violent Video Games on Self-Control, Cheating, and Aggression," *Social Psychological and Personality Science* 5, no. 4 (May 2014): 451-8, doi: 10.1177/1948550613509286.

18. Angie S. Page et al., "Children's Screen Viewing Is Related to Psychological Difficulties Irrespective of Physical Activity," *Pediatrics* 126, no. 5 (November 2010): 1011-17, doi: 10.1542/peds.2010-1154.

Chapter 4—Meditation: On Keeping Quiet

1. Xiao Ma et al., "The Effect of Diaphragmatic Breathing on Attention, Negative Affect and Stress in Healthy Adults," *Frontiers in Psychology* 8 (June 2017), doi: 10.3389/fpsyg.2017.00874.

2. Adele Ahlberg Calhoun, *Spiritual Disciplines Handbook*: Practices that Transform Us (Downers Grove: IVP Books, 2005), 172.

3. Richard J. Foster, *Celebration of Discipline: The Path to Spiritual Growth* (New York: HarperCollins, 1998), 31.

4. Tim Challies, "A Danger of Lectio Divina," *Challies*, May 21, 2104, https://www.challies.com/articles/a-danger-of-lectio-divina/.

5. Deborah Weatherspoon, "Box Breathing," *Healthline*, February 22, 2019, https://www.healthline.com/health/box-breathing.

Chapter 5—Studying God's Word: Learning to Feed Ourselves

1. Voddie Baucham, Bob Lepine, and Dennis Rainey, "Leading Your Family in Faith," *FamilyLife Today*, February 26, 2008, https://www.familylife.com/podcast/familylife-today/leading-your-family-in-faith/.

2. Jessica Thompson, "Help Wanted: Looking for Someone to Make My Kids Love the Bible," *Crossway*, July 22, 2014, https://www.crossway.org/blog/2014/07/help-wanted-looking-for-someone-to-make-my-kids-love-the-bible/.

Chapter 6—Simplicity: When Less Is So Much More

1. Randy Alcorn, *The Treasure Principle* (Colorado Springs: Multnomah, 2005), 34.
2. Richard J. Foster, *Celebration of Discipline: The Path to Spiritual Growth* (New York: HarperCollins, 1998), 79-80.
3. Johnathon Bowers, "America's Most Tolerated Sin," *Desiring God*, February 18, 2015, https://www.desiringgod.org/messages/americas-most-tolerated-sin.
4. John Piper, *A Hunger for God* (Wheaton, IL: Crossway, 1997).
5. Valerie E. Hess and Marti Watson Garlett, *Habits of a Child's Heart: Raising Your Kids with the Spiritual Disciplines* (Colorado Springs: NavPress, 2004), 51.
6. This term was coined by Kosuke Koyama in *Three Mile an Hour God* (London: SCM Press, 2015).
7. Dallas Willard, as cited in John Ortberg, *Soul Keeping: Caring for the Most Important Part of You* (Grand Rapids: Zondervan, 2014), 20.

Chapter 7—Holy Sexuality: We Are Worth More Than This

1. Christopher Asmus, "Longing for Intimacy: Four Promises for Same-Sex-Attracted Christians," *Desiring God*, January 18, 2018, https://www.desiringgod.org/articles/longing-for-intimacy.
2. Morgan Bennett, "The New Narcotic," *The Public Discourse*, October 9, 2013, https://www.thepublicdiscourse.com/2013/10/10846/.
3. Ibid.
4. Cameron Cole, "Four Things Youth Workers Would Tell Parents About Teenagers, Social Media, and Technology," *Core Christianity*, April 2, 2019, https://corechristianity.com/resource-library/articles/four-things-youth-workers-would-tell-parents-about-teenagers-social-media-and-technology.
5. Nellie Bowles, "A Dark Consensus About Screens and Kids Begins to Emerge in Silicon Valley," *New York Times*, October 26, 2018, https://www.nytimes.com/2018/10/26/style/phones-children-silicon-valley.html.
6. Find instructions for iPhones at https://www.iphonefaq.org/archives/972265 and for Androids at https://www.wikihow.com/Block-Multimedia-Messages-(MMS)-on-Android.
7. Kempton Turner, "Pure Pleasure: The Battle for Sexual Purity," The Gospel Coalition, 2020, https://www.thegospelcoalition.org/course/pure-pleasure-the-battle-for-sexual-purity/#feast-and-fences.
8. Juli Slattery, "Pursue Wholeness, not Purity," *Java with Juli*, July 20, 2019.
9. Lauren Winner, *Mudhouse Sabbath: An Invitation to a Life of Spiritual Discipline* (Brewster, MA: Paraclete, 2007), 67.
10. Nsikan Akpan, "In Kavanaugh Debate, 'Boys Will Be Boys' Is an Unscientific Excuse for Assault," PBS.com, September 21, 2018, https://www.pbs.org/newshour/science/why-boys-will-be-boys-is-an-unscientific-excuse-for-assault.

11. "Facts About Suicide," *The Trevor Project*, https://www.thetrevorproject.org/resources /preventing-suicide/facts-about-suicide/#sm.0000h4jwmy7gpflazah2hmzp2lnjr, accessed July 6, 2020.

12. Modified from "Helping Teens Resist Sexual Pressure," HealthyChildren.org, November 2, 2009, https://www.healthychildren.org/English/ages-stages/teen/dating-sex /Pages/Helping-Teens-Resist-Sexual-Pressure.aspx.

13. Janel Breitenstein, "Casual Sex: What's in It for Her?" FamilyLife.com, 2019, https:// www.familylife.com/articles/topics/life-issues/challenges/cultural-issues/casual-sex -whats-in-it-for-her/.

Chapter 8—Community: Almost Home

1. John Lynch, Bruce McNicol, and Bill Thrall, *The Cure: What If God Isn't Who You Think He Is and Neither Are You?* (Phoenix, AZ: Trueface, 2011), 19.

2. Johann Hari, *Lost Connections: Uncovering the Real Causes of Depression—and the Unexpected Solutions* (New York: Bloomsbury, 2018), 79.

3. Ibid., 59.

4. John and Stasi Eldredge, *Captivating: Unveiling the Mystery of a Woman's Soul,* revised and updated (Nashville: Thomas Nelson, 2011).

5. Drew Hunter, *Made for Friendship: The Relationship That Halves Our Sorrows and Doubles Our Joys* (Wheaton: Crossway, 2018), 34-36.

6. Revised from similar concept by Jamie Miller, *10-Minute Life Lessons for Kids: 52 Fun and Simple Games and Activities to Teach Your Children Honesty, Trust, Love, and Other Important Values* (New York: HarperPerennial, 1998), 147.

Chapter 9—Discernment: Sorting the Skittles

1. Aleksandr Solzhenitsyn, *The Gulag Archipelago: An Experiment in Literary Investigation,* trans. Thomas P. Whitney (New York: HarperCollins, 2007), 75.

2. Joyce Slayton, "The Mandalorian TV Review," *Common Sense Media,* https://www .commonsensemedia.org/tv-reviews/the-mandalorian.

Chapter 10—Service: Downward Mobility

1. "Where Do We Go from Here?" (1967), as cited in https://mbird.com/2020/01/how -mlk-got-his-name/, January 20, 2020.

2. Richard J. Foster, *Celebration of Discipline: The Path to Spiritual Growth* (New York: HarperCollins, 1998).

3. "We must confess, dirty clothes make a mess!" KidsOfIntegrity.com. https://www .kidsofintegrity.com/lessons/righteousness/hands-options/we-must-confess-dirty -clothes-make-mess.

4. C.S. Lewis, *Mere Christianity* (New York: HarperOne, 2015), 112.

Chapter 11—Sharing Our Faith: Loving Them This Much

1. Ruth Haley Barton, *Life Together in Christ: Experiencing Transformation in Community* (Downers Grove, IL: InterVarsity Press, 2014), 153.

2. Esther Katende-Magezi, "The Impact of Second-Hand Clothes and Shoes in East Africa," Geneva, Switzerland: Cuts International, Geneva (2017), http://www.cuts -geneva.org/pdf/PACT2-STUDY-The_Impact_of_Second_Hand_Clothes_and_Shoes _in_East_Africa.pdf.

3. As cited in Justin Taylor, "How Much Do You Have to Hate Somebody to *Not* Proselytize?" TheGospelCoalition.org. November 18, 2009, https://www.thegospelcoalition .org/blogs/justin-taylor/how-much-do-you-have-to-hate-somebody-to-not-proselytize/.

4. Ibid.

5. These questions are based on https://goexplorethebible.com/uncategorized/10-questions -to-initiate-a-spiritual-conversation/.

6. Qur'an 50:16.

Chapter 12—Resilience: Your Child, Stronger

1. Mary Bates, "Super Powers for the Blind and Deaf," *The Scientific American*, September 18, 2012, https://www.scientificamerican.com/article/superpowers-for-the-blind-and -deaf/.

2. Timothy Keller, *Every Good Endeavor: Connecting Your Work to God's Work* (New York: Viking, 2012), 154.

3. "Apple 1 from 1976 Signed by Wozniak Sells for $650,000," BBC, May 25, 2013, https://www.bbc.com/news/technology-22667353.

4. Michael Card, *A Sacred Sorrow: Reaching Out to God in the Lost Language of Lament* (Colorado Springs: NavPress, 2005), 31.

5. Timothy Keller, "Real Bad," *Daily Keller: Wisdom from Tim Keller 365 Days a Year,* February 12, 2015, http://dailykeller.com/real-bad/.

6. Brené Brown, *Daring Greatly: How the Courage to Be Vulnerable Transforms the Way We Live, Love, Parent, and Lead* (New York: Penguin Random House, 2012), 239.

7. Thomas Keating, *The Human Condition: Contemplation and Transformation* (Mahwah, NJ: Paulist, 1999), 38.

8. Jamie Miller, *10-Minute Life Lessons for Kids: 52 Fun and Simple Games and Activities to Teach Your Children Honesty, Trust, Love, and Other Important Values* (New York: HarperPerennial, 1998), 60-61.

9. Ibid., 48.

10. J. Scott Duvall, "Angry at Death: Reading John 11," EverydayBioethics.org, January 24, 2017, https://everydaybioethics.org/intersections/angry-death-reading-john-11.

Chapter 13—Respecting Authority: Stepping Down

1. Tedd Tripp, *Shepherding a Child's Heart* (Wapwollopen, PA: Shepherd, 2005), 4-5.

2. John and Stacy Lynch, Bruce and Janet McNicol, and Bill and Grace Thrall, *The Cure & Parents* (Phoenix: TrueFace, 2016), 12.

3. Ginger Hubbard, *Don't Make Me Count to Three: A Mom's Look at Heart-Oriented Discipline* (Wapwallopen, PA: Shepherd, 2004), 117.

4. Gretchen Rubin, "Habit Strategies and Tips for Rebels," *Gretchen Rubin,* August 8, 2017, https://gretchenrubin.com/2017/08/four-tendencies-rebels-habits/.

Chapter 14—Confession and Repentance: Regrets Only

1. Ken Sande with Tom Raabe, *Peacemaking for Families* (Colorado Springs: Focus on the Family, 2002), 57.

2. Paul David Tripp, *New Morning Mercies: A Daily Gospel Devotional* (Wheaton: Crossway, 2014), August 11.

3. Corlette Sande, *The Young Peacemaker: Teaching Students to Respond to Conflict in God's Way* (Wapwallopen, PA: Shepherd Press Inc., 2002).

4. Altered from "Object Lesson About Confession," iFindSermons. https://www.youtube.com/watch?v=bFa4FEGSUe4.

Chapter 15—Adoration: The Song That Never Ends

1. Dennis Rainey, e-mail message to author, December 20, 2015.

2. C.S. Lewis, *Reflections on the Psalms* (Boston, MA: Harcourt, 1958), 90.

3. Amy Fallon, "Uganda Motorbike Deaths: Concerns Grow over Silent Killers," *The Guardian*, August 13, 2013, https://www.theguardian.com/global-development/2013/aug/13/uganda-motorbike-deaths-road-safety-boda-bodas.

4. "Giving Thanks Can Make You Happier," *Harvard Health Publishing*, accessed October 9, 2020, https://www.health.harvard.edu/healthbeat/giving-thanks-can-make-you-happier.

5. Jerusha Clark, "The Gift of Gratitude," *Axis Culture Translator* 5, no. 48 (November 17, 2019), https://axis.org/culture-translators/vol-5-issue-48-nov-27-2019.

6. Elizabeth Berg, *Dream When You're Feeling Blue* (New York: Ballantine, 2008), 141.

7. Ann Voskamp, "(14 Ways) How to Raise Grateful, Thankful, Joyful Kids: When You're Tired of Kids Complaining," *A Holy Experience,* November 21, 2019, https://annvoskamp.com/2019/11/14-ways-how-to-raise-grateful-thankful-joy-filled-kids-when-youre-tired-of-kids-complaining/.

8. Shane Claiborne, Enuma Okoro, and Jonathan Wilson-Hartgrove, *Common Prayer: A Liturgy for Ordinary Radicals* (Grand Rapids: Zondervan, 2010), 116.

Group Discussion Guide

1. Joyce Huggett, *Spiritual Classics: Selected Readings on the Twelve Spiritual Disciplines* (New York: HarperOne, 2007), 11.

To learn more about Harvest House books and
to read sample chapters, visit our website:

www.harvesthousepublishers.com

HARVEST HOUSE PUBLISHERS
EUGENE, OREGON